RIO DE JANEIRO

MICHAEL SOMMERS

Contents

Rio de Janeiro

Highlights

★ **Corcovado:** Crowned by the all-embracing statue of Christ the Redeemer, "Hunchback" mountain was recently voted one of the Seven Modern Wonders of the World (page 20).

★ **Pão de Açúcar:** One of Rio's most instantly recognizable icons, this monumental chunk of sugar loaf-shaped granite rises out of the Baía de Guanabara (page 21).

★ **Copacabana Beach:** Urban beaches don't get any more dazzling than this gorgeous arc of sugary fine sand that is a microcosm unto itself (page 22).

★ **Ipanema and Leblon:** More than just fabulous beaches, these two adjacent neighborhoods are the eternal epitome of Carioca cool, with shady streets, bars, boutiques, restaurants, and a bossa nova vibe (page 23).

★ **Carnaval:** Samba the day and night away for five days at Rio's spectacularly hedonistic *festa* to end all *festas* (page 29).

★ **Floresta da Tijuca:** Brazil's largest urban park, Floresta da Tijuca is a lush green oasis of native Atlantic forest that is perfect for a refreshing getaway (page 42).

★ **Museu Imperial:** The former summer residence of Dom Pedro II, located in Petrópolis, offers a glimpse into the life of an emperor in the tropics (page 61).

★ **Búzios:** Brazil's version of Saint-Tropez is a tropical chic playground with sophisticated amenities, a celebrated nightlife, and beaches for every taste under the sun (page 69).

★ **Ilha Grande:** The largest of the many islands in the Bay of Angra dos Reis, Ilha Grande is an island paradise that captures the essence and ethos of "back to nature" (page 74).

★ **Paraty:** One of the most charming and best-preserved Portuguese colonial towns in Brazil is surrounded by breathtaking mountains and idyllic beaches (page 77).

E ven if you've never been, it's easy to hear "Rio" and automatically conjure up its postcard sights: the *Christ the Redeemer* statue atop lush Corcovado, the sweeping white crescent of Copacabana beach, and Pão de Açúcar.

When you do finally arrive, it's a shock—these landmarks are even more impressive in real life. After all, this is the city that Cariocas (residents of Rio) refer to proudly as the *Cidade Maravilhosa* (Marvelous City).

Like many a modern tourist, Brazil's imperial family enjoyed Rio to the hilt, but when they couldn't stand the heat, they literally took to the hills. Emperor Pedro II went so far as to build an ornate pink summer palace (now a fascinating museum) in the mountains. Only an hour from Rio—but usually 5-10 degrees cooler—Petrópolis, Teresópolis, and other neighboring towns continue to offer refuge to vacationers who can take advantage of sophisticated amenities surrounded by majestic scenery. When nature beckons, the national parks of Serra dos Órgãos and Itatiaia are close by with their orchid-laced hiking trails winding through native Atlantic forest.

Natural attractions are also in abundance along the coasts of Rio de Janeiro state. East of the city are the upscale resort towns of Cabo Frio and Búzios, which offer beautiful sandy beaches with calm pools for snorkeling and big waves for surfers. Búzios is particularly charming, with cobblestoned streets and shades of Saint-Tropez. Those in search of more tranquil options can head south along the Costa Verde (Green Coast), named for the verdant mountains that provide a striking backdrop to the unspoiled beaches. Highlights along this coast include the island paradise of Ilha Grande and the beautifully preserved colonial town of Paraty.

PLANNING YOUR TIME

One week will give you time to explore museums and historic sights, shop, and lounge on the city's famous beaches as well as take a day trip or two to the surrounding beaches or mountains of Rio de Janeiro state. Despite the great variety of its attractions, Rio de Janeiro

---

Previous: Ipanema beach; the waterfront of Ipanema and Copacabana Beach. **Above:** Pão de Açúcar

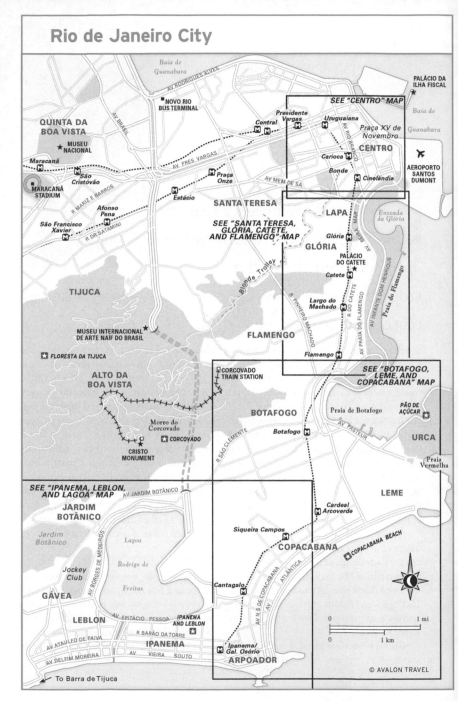

Rio de Janeiro City

Baía de Guanabara

AV RODRIGUES ALVES

PALÁCIO DA ILHA FISCAL

NOVO RIO BUS TERMINAL

SEE "CENTRO" MAP

Baía de Guanabara

AV BRASIL

QUINTA DA BOA VISTA

★ MUSEU NACIONAL

Maracanã

MARACANÃ STADIUM

São Cristóvão

R MARIZ E BARROS

Afonso Pena

São Francisco Xavier

R DR SATAMINI

Central

Presidente Vargas

AV. PRES. VARGAS

Praça Onze

Estácio

AV MEM DE SÁ

Uruguaiana

AV. RIO BRANCO

Praça XV de Novembro

CENTRO

Carioca

Bonde

Cinelândia

AEROPORTO SANTOS DUMONT

SANTA TERESA

LAPA

SEE "SANTA TERESA, GLÓRIA, CATETE, AND FLAMENGO" MAP

Glória

GLÓRIA

PALÁCIO DO CATETE ★

Enseada da Glória

AV BEIRA MAR

Catete

Blonde Trolley

TIJUCA

MUSEU INTERNACIONAL DE ARTE NAÏF DO BRASIL ★

FLORESTA DA TIJUCA

R. PINHEIRO MACHADO

Largo do Machado

R. DO CATETE

FLAMENGO

Flamengo

AV PRAIA DO FLAMENGO

AV INFANTE DOM HENRIQUE

Praia do Flamengo

ALTO DA BOA VISTA

CORCOVADO TRAIN STATION

SEE "BOTAFOGO, LEME, AND COPACABANA" MAP

PÃO DE AÇÚCAR

BOTAFOGO

Praia de Botafogo

Morro do Corcovado

CORCOVADO

R. SÃO CLEMENTE

Botafogo

AV PASTEUR

URCA

★ CRISTO MONUMENT

Praia Vermelha

SEE "IPANEMA, LEBLON, AND LAGOA" MAP

AV JARDIM BOTÂNICO

JARDIM BOTÂNICO

LEME

Jardim Botânico

Lagoa Rodrigo de Freitas

AV BORGES DE MEDEIROS

Cardeal Arcoverde

Siqueira Campos

Jockey Club

COPACABANA

COPACABANA BEACH

GÁVEA

LEBLON

AV EPITÁCIO PESSOA

IPANEMA AND LEBLON

Cantagalo

AV N S DE COPACABANA

AV ATLÂNTICA

AV ATAULFO DE PAIVA

R BARÃO DA TORRE

IPANEMA

0   1 mi

AV DELFIM MOREIRA

AV VIEIRA SOUTO

Ipanema/ Gal. Osório

0   1 km

ARPOADOR

→ To Barra de Tijuca

© AVALON TRAVEL

state is compact, and most sights are only two or three hours away. While some of these destinations (such as Petrópolis and Teresópolis) can be visited as day trips from Rio, it would be a crime to rush when faced with such intense natural beauty and relaxing environs. Two or three days reserved for the mountains surrounding Petrópolis and Itatiaia and another couple (at least) for the beautiful beaches of Búzios and Arraial do Cabo (north of Rio) or Ilha Grande and Paraty (south of Rio) will give you adequate time to unwind and explore.

There are several factors to consider when planning a trip. In **summer** (Dec.-early Mar.), Rio sizzles—both figuratively (festivities and nightlife are at their zenith) and literally (with temperatures hovering around 40°C/104°F

and lots of sticky humidity). Make sure you have an air-conditioned hotel, or head for the much cooler hills. Another option is to visit in **winter** (June-Sept.), when the sun is less intense and the beaches won't be quite so crowded (at least during the week). Nights are comfortably cool (15-20°C/60-70°F). The cold fronts that come up from Argentina, bringing cool winds and rain that can last for two or three days, are the only thing to watch out for. Rio enjoys a considerable amount of precipitation throughout the year; December to March, rains are particularly frequent. To take part in either of Rio's most famous and fabulous festivities—Réveillon (New Year's Eve) and Carnaval—prepare to have deep pockets and to make flight and hotel bookings months in advance.

Rio de Janeiro City

Rio's setting is incomparable: This tropical metropolis of 8 million is both urban and urbane, yet every street seems to end in an explosion of towering green or a soothing slice of blue. The 500-year-old city is also hardly lacking in impressive architecture. Its downtown is a treasure trove of baroque churches, imperial palaces (many converted into cultural centers), and monumental buildings and squares. History of a more recent variety is present in the Zona Sul neighborhoods of Copacabana, Ipanema, and Leblon; all three are famed for the stunning white-sand beaches that serve as playgrounds for Cariocas and tourists from all walks of life. It was here that bossa nova was born and the bikini made its mark. Despite all the beautiful people, Zona Sul retains a relaxed casualness that is typical of Rio. Sip a fresh tropical nectar at a juice bar or enjoy an icy beer at one of many rustic bars known as *botequins,* and watch as barefoot surfer boys and bikini girls in Havaianas stroll through the streets.

While daytime in Rio is languid, nighttime sizzles with possibilities. For dinner, choose

from a profusion of world-class restaurants. Then either chill at a swanky Zona Sul lounge, dance, drink, and flirt at a nightclub, or join the pulsating throngs in the historic *bairros* of Lapa, Saúde, and Gamboa, who flock to listen to live *chorinho, forró,* and, of course, samba.

Speaking of samba, it's impossible to mention Rio without alluding to the world-famous extravaganza known as Carnaval. It doesn't matter whether you take in the parades at the Sambódromo, dance through the streets with a traditional neighborhood *bloco* (Carnaval group), or merely make it to one of the *escola de samba* (samba school) rehearsals held throughout the year. The Carnaval spirit is highly contagious. Like Rio itself, it will leave you wanting more.

ORIENTATION

What's left of Rio's colonial past and most of its churches and museums are concentrated in its old downtown core, known as **Centro**. However, beaches, shopping, restaurants, nightlife, and most hotels—as well as access to the Floresta da Tijuca—are in the more upscale **Zona Sul** neighborhoods. The area north of Centro is known as the **Zona Norte.** This vast urban zone is home to Rio's lower-class neighborhoods and encompasses the Rodoviária Novo Rio (bus station), Aeroporto Internacional Tom Jobim (Galeão), and Maracanã soccer stadium.

Despite Rio's sprawl, getting around the Centro and Zona Sul neighborhoods is fairly easy. An excellent Metrô service links Zona Norte, Centro, Flamengo, Botafogo, Copacabana, and Ipanema, and an efficiently integrated Metrô-express and standard bus service allows you to easily access other neighborhoods, including Cosme Velho, Leblon, Gávea, Jardim Botânico, São Conrado, and Barra. Walking is a wonderful way to explore the city. During the day, it's quite safe to stroll around (with the exception of Centro on weekends). At night more care should be taken, although most Zona Sul neighborhoods are quite bright and busy until at least 10pm.

SIGHTS
Centro
Centro refers to Rio's historic downtown commercial district, where cobblestoned alleys, grand baroque churches, turn-of-the-20th-century architecture, and the ubiquitous high-rises and urban chaos of a 21st-century megalopolis make up a fascinating patchwork. As an antidote to the upscale beach culture of Zona Sul, pockets of the Centro are quite interesting, particularly if you want to get a sense of Rio's rich past.

Despite the traffic, navigating the area is quite easy on foot. Centro is also well served by buses from both the Zona Sul and Zona Norte (take anything marked Centro, Praça XV, or Praça Mauá) and by Metrô (the most convenient stations are Cinelândia, Carioca, Uruguaiana, Presidente Vargas, and Praça Onze). During the day and into the early evening Centro is usually jam-packed, but at night and on weekends the area is a ghost town and quite unsafe to stroll around. If taking in an exhibition or performance during these times, it's best to take a taxi.

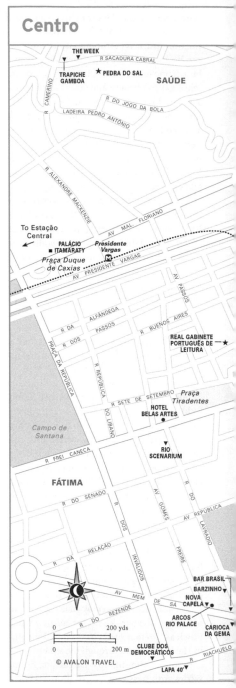

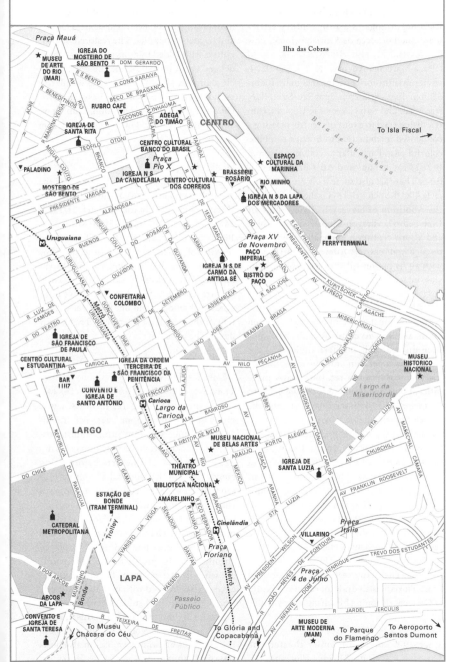

MUSEU HISTÓRICO NACIONAL

One of the few surviving constructions from Rio's beginnings as a 16th-century settlement, the Fortaleza de Santiago (1603), now houses the **Museu Histórico Nacional** (Praça Marechal Âncora, tel. 21/2550-9224, www.museuhistoriconacional.com.br, 10am-5:30pm Tues.-Fri., 2pm-6pm Sat.-Sun., R$6, free Wed. and Sun.). A visit to this museum is a fitting start to a tour of Centro, offering a condensed introduction to Brazil's complex, colorful past. Particular attention is given to Brazil's indigenous and Afro-Brazilian cultures. There are also some truly precious artifacts, like the pen Princesa Isabel used to sign the Abolition of Slavery in 1888, Emperor Dom Pedro II's dragon-capped golden throne, and a 19th-century homeopathic pharmacy, rescued in its entirety from a street in Centro with all its potion-filled crystal and opaline vials intact.

CINELÂNDIA

Although most of Centro's traffic-laden main avenue, Avenida Rio Branco, has been disfigured by modern high-rises, the stretch that opens up onto the monumental **Praça Floriano** has retained many magnificent buildings, among them the Theatro Municipal, the Biblioteca Nacional, and the Museu Nacional de Belas Artes.

The area encompassing Praça Floriano is known as **Cinelândia**. In the 1920s, ambitious plans existed to turn this elegant plaza into a Carioca version of Broadway—only instead of theaters, movie palaces were built, including Rio's first cinemas. Only one of these glamorous art deco palaces is still intact—the Cine Odeon Petrobras—while the rest were snatched up by churches, such as the Igreja Universal de Deus (Universal Kingdom of God). The many cafés scattered around Praça Floriano still draw an eclectic mixture of Cariocas dropping by during happy hour.

THEATRO MUNICIPAL

Since 1909, Brazil's premier theater, the **Theatro Municipal** (Praça Floriano, tel. 21/2332-9134, www.theatromunicipal.rj.gov. br), has played host to some of the world's most prestigious orchestras and opera, dance, and theater companies. The restored interior glitters with gilded mirrors and crystal chandeliers. Onyx banisters line the grand marble staircase, and there are some wonderful mosaic frescoes and stained-glass windows. Guided tours are offered (noon, 2pm, 3pm, and 4pm Tues.-Fri., 11am, noon, and 1pm Sat., R$10).

BIBLIOTECA NACIONAL

The largest library in Latin America and the eighth largest in the world, Rio's **Biblioteca Nacional** (Av. Rio Branco 219, tel. 21/2220-9484, www.bn.br, 10am-5pm Mon.-Fri., 10am-2pm Sat.) boasts some 13 million tomes, the first of which were brought to Brazil by Dom João VI in 1808. Completed in 1910, the building is an eclectic fusion of neoclassical and art nouveau styles. You don't have to be a serious bibliophile to opt for a free guided tour of the grandiose interior, offered hourly during the week.

MUSEU NACIONAL DE BELAS ARTES

The **Museu Nacional de Belas Artes** (Av. Rio Branco 199, tel. 21/2240-0068, www. mnba.gov.br, 10am-6pm Tues.-Fri., noon-5pm Sat.-Sun., R$8, free Sun.) is an imposing neoclassical temple that housed Rio's national school of fine arts before being converted into this somewhat somber museum. It has a modest collection of European works, but you should really focus your attention on the national collection, which provides an excellent overview of 19th- and 20th-century Brazilian painting. Displayed chronologically, highlights include painters who, departing from European influences, experimented with new and distinctly Brazilian styles and subject matter, including Anita Malfatti, Cândido Portinari, Lasar Segall, and Alfredo Volpi. A gallery displays Brazilian folk art, and the museum also hosts traveling exhibitions.

Following Avenida Rio Branco north brings you to **Largo** and **Rua da Carioca**, a bustling area filled vendors and a maze of cobblestoned streets. You will immediately be impressed by the monumental hillside complex of the Igreja de São Francisco da Penitência and the Convento de Santo Antônio.

CONVENTO DE SANTO ANTÔNIO

Built in the early 1600s to house Franciscan monks, the **Convento de Santo Antônio** (Largo da Carioca, tel. 21/2262-0129, 8am-6pm Mon.-Fri., 8am-11am Sat.) is one of Rio's oldest surviving buildings. Although most of the church was been modified, you can admire some baroque works and a finely wrought sacristy panel of blue-and-white Portuguese azulejos (ceramic tiles) illustrating the life of Santo Antônio.

IGREJA DE SÃO FRANCISCO DA PENITÊNCIA

The interior of the **Igreja de São Francisco da Penitência** (Largo da Carioca, tel. 21/2262-0197, 9am-4pm Tues.-Fri., R$2), one of Rio's most sumptuous baroque jewels, may blind you by the sheer amount of pure gold on display—400 kilograms (880 pounds), to be precise. While the church took 115 years to build (construction began in 1657), the final 30 years were almost exclusively dedicated to covering the beautifully sculpted cedar altars and naves in gold.

REAL GABINETE PORTUGUÊS DE LEITURA

Stylized sailors' knots, seashells, and Moorish motifs mark the facade of the **Real Gabinete Português de Leitura** (Rua Luís de Camões 30, tel. 21/2221-3138, www.realgabinete.com. br, 9am-6pm Mon.-Fri., free). Inside is a large library of works in the Portuguese language and a stunning reading room with mile-high ceilings, jacaranda tables, and seemingly endless polished wood bookshelves. To get here from the Largo da Carioca, walk down Rua da Carioca to Praça Tiradentes, then take a right on Avenida Passos.

PRAÇA XV

Historically, Praça XV comprised the symbolic heart of Centro. Its full name, **Praça XV de Novembro,** refers to November 15, 1899, the day when Brazil's first president, Manuel Deodoro de Fonseca, declared Brazil a republic. Many significant historical events have taken place here—among them the crowning of Brazil's two emperors, Pedro I and Pedro II, and the abolition of slavery in 1888.

PAÇO IMPERIAL

Praça XV once served as a large public patio to the stately **Paço (Palácio) Imperial** (Praça XV de Novembro 48, tel. 21/2215-2622, www. pacoimperial.com.br, 11am-7pm Tues.-Sun., free). Built in 1743, the palace was a residence for Portugal's colonial governors; it then housed the Portuguese court when Dom João VI fled Napoleon's forces in 1808. Today, it contains temporary exhibits of contemporary art. Overlooking the internal courtyard is a lovely café and restaurant, the Bistrô do Paço, as well as Arlequim, an excellent book and music store that often hosts pocket shows.

Directly across Praça XV from the Paço Imperial, an impressive arch leads down the **Beco de Telles,** a cobblestoned alley lined with elegant 19th-century buildings. Wander down this street and the equally narrow and atmospheric Travessa do Comércio, Rua Visconde de Itaboraí, and Rua Ouvidor to get a sense of what Rio was like in the 18th and 19th centuries.

IGREJA NOSSA SENHORA DE CARMO DA ANTIGA SÉ

The **Igreja Nossa Senhora de Carmo da Antiga Sé** (Rua Sete de Setembro 14, tel. 21/2242-7766, 7am-4pm Mon.-Fri., free) sits across from Praça XV. Constructed in 1761, it served as Rio's principal cathedral until 1980. Many of the city's major religious commemorations—including Emperor Pedro I's coronation and the baptism and marriage of Emperor Pedro II—were celebrated here. Serious history buffs should check out the sound-and-light show (1:30pm Tues.-Fri., noon and 1pm Sat., 12:30 and 1pm Sun., R$8), in which a holographic priest recounts the church's history. A small museum (10am-3:30pm Tues.-Fri., 11am-2pm Sat.-Sun., R$5) displays vestiges of the original 16th-century chapel along with a crypt containing the remains of Brazil's "discoverer," Pedro Álvares Cabral.

ESPAÇO CULTURAL DA MARINHA AND THE ILHA FISCAL

Along the waterfront, the Espaço Cultural da Marinha (Av. Alfred Agache, near Praça XV, tel. 21/2233-9165, www.mar.mil.br, noon-5pm Tues.-Sun., free) features a small collection of antique maps, navigating equipment, and buried treasure rescued from sunken ships in the Baía de Guanabara, offering an engaging glimpse of Brazil's maritime history. Kids will have fun clambering about on the World War II-era torpedo destroyer and a cool 1970s submarine, both moored outside the main building.

From here, you can take a guided trip by boat or minibus across the bay to the Ilha Fiscal, the site of a neo-Gothic castle that once housed a customs collection center. The extravagant construction resembles something out of a fairy tale: It was here that the last legendary royal ball of the Brazilian empire was held—one week before the declaration of Brazil as a republic. Boat trips depart at 12:30pm, 2pm, and 3:30pm Thurs.-Sun. Tours (R$20) last 1.5 hours.

IGREJA NOSSA SENHORA DA CANDELÁRIA

You can't miss the monumental Igreja Nossa Senhora da Candelária (Praça Pio X, tel. 21/2233-2324, 7:30am-4pm Mon.-Fri., 8am-noon Sat., 9am-1pm Sun., free). Begun in 1775, the present church took more than 100 years to complete, which accounts for its mixture of baroque and Renaissance elements. Ceiling panels recount the legend of the original 16th-century chapel's construction by a shipwrecked captain whose life was miraculously saved.

IGREJA DO MOSTEIRO DE SÃO BENTO

Located north of Praça Mauá, the Igreja do Mosteiro de São Bento (Rua Dom Geraldo 68, tel. 21/2206-8100, 7am-6pm daily) is Rio's most magnificent example of baroque architecture. Instead of being blindingly ostentatious, the lavish gold interior has a warm and burnished hue, the result of soft lighting used to preserve the precious artwork (which includes some exceptionally fine sculpted saints and painted panels). On Sunday morning you can take part in the 10am mass, in which the Benedictine monks chant Gregorian hymns accompanied by an organ (arrive early if you want a seat.). Access to the monastery is via an elevator located at Rua Dom Geraldo 40.

MUSEU DE ARTE DO RIO

The Museu de Arte do Rio (Praça Mauá 5, tel. 21/2203-1235, www.museudeartedorio. org.br, 10am-5pm Tues.-Sun., R$8, free Tues.) is one of the more promising symbols of the transformation and revitalization of Rio's historic port district. A futuristic roof of curvaceous concrete and a suspended walkway unite two completely antithetical buildings: the 19th-century eclectic-style Palacete Dom João VI and a 1950s modernist-style bus terminal. Within the former are four floors devoted to permanent and temporary exhibits focusing on art related to Rio. Windows offer ample opportunities for sea-gazing; hence the aptness of the museum's acronym, MAR (ocean).

Zona Norte

When traveling from the Tom Jobim international airport to Centro or Zona Sul, you'll get your first sight of Rio's sprawling Zona Norte district. The area is largely residential, with working-class and poor neighborhoods alongside vast *favelas*. Poverty and drug-related violence make large pockets extremely unsafe. The exception is the Quinta da Boa Vista (fairly close to Centro and easily accessible by Metrô), a vast park with some sights, among them the Museu Nacional. If you have

Port Revival

Rio's Port Zone stretches north from Praça Mauá, encompassing the *bairros* of Saúde and Gamboa. Occupation of these *bairros* dates back to early colonial days, when aristocrats built villas along the hillsides overlooking the beach-fringed Baía da Guanabara. In the late 1700s, the beaches vanished, as did the well-to-do residents, when the Cais de Valongo replaced Praça XV as the city's disembarkation point for the more than 1 million African slaves who would arrive in Rio over the next century. Those that survived the voyage (on average less than half) were taken to *casas de engorda* ("fattening houses") to gain weight before being sold at the Mercado Valongo, which during the 19th century was the largest slave market in the world.

While waiting to be hauled off to gold mines and coffee plantations, slaves congregated in the square known as Largo de São Francisco da Prainha, where they chanted and beat rhythms on improvised drums—resulting in the birth of Rio's samba. Numerous elements of African culture persevered, earning the port zone the nickname "Little Africa." Following the abolition of slavery, many free slaves from Bahia migrated to the area and began settling on the hillside known as Morro da Providência. Considered Rio's first *favela*, this community still retains its strong Afro-Brazilian roots.

The Port Zone had been neglected until, spurred on by the 2014 World Cup and 2016 Olympics, the area was earmarked for a major overhaul. Baptized Porto Maravilha, the massive revitalization project plans to improve existing communities and create new ones by investing in residential, commercial, and cultural spaces, such as the **Museu de Arte do Rio** and the completed **Museu de Amanhã** (Museum of Tomorrow).

There's also been a movement to highlight the area's past as a cradle of Afro-Brazilian culture. Saúde and Gamboa have become hot spots to hear traditional samba, particularly in the picturesque square known as Pedra do Sal, where *samba de rodas* erupt every Monday and Friday night. A **Historical and Archaeological Circuit Celebrating African Heritage** (http://portomaravilha. com.br/circuito) allows visitors to investigate historically important sites.

some extra time to kill, you can combine its attractions into a day trip.

QUINTA DA BOA VISTA AND MUSEU NACIONAL

A former sugar plantation, the **Quinta da Boa Vista** (Av. Pedro II between Rua Almirante Baltazar and Rua Dom Meinrado, São Cristóvão, 9am-4:30pm Tues.-Sun.) was where Brazil's imperial family took up residence between 1822 and 1889. The expansive grounds feature tree-lined walkways, flower gardens, lakes, and even a zoo.

The emperors lived in the stately neoclassical Palácio de São Cristóvão, now home to the **Museu Nacional** (tel. 21/2562-6901, www. museunacional.ufrj.br, 10am-4pm Tues.-Sun., R$3). Brazil's oldest scientific museum houses an enormous, somewhat dusty collection started by Dom João VI. The archaeological section focuses on prehistoric Latin American peoples, while the ethnological collection has

some artifacts related to Brazil's indigenous cultures. Among the highlights is the Bendigo Meteorite, which landed in the state of Bahia in 1888 and is the heaviest metallic mass ever known to have crashed through the planet's atmosphere. To get to the Quinta da Boa Vista, take the Metrô to São Cristóvão.

FEIRA DE SÃO CRISTÓVÃO

Near the Quinta da Boa Vista is the traditional **Feira de São Cristóvão** (Pavilhão de São Cristóvão, São Cristóvão, tel. 21/2580-5335, www.feiradesaocristovao.org.br, 10am-6pm Tues.-Thurs., 10am-10pm Fri.-Sun., R$3). Also known as the Centro Luiz Gonzaga de Tradições Nordestinas, this massive outdoor market has 700 *barracas* (stalls), where vendors hawk products ranging from handwoven hammocks from Ceará and leather hats and sandals from the sunbaked Sertão to jars of herb-infused *cachaças* from Bahia. Tuesday-Thursday you'll find lots of places for typical lunches. The good times don't really roll, however, until the weekends, when the *barracas* stay open around the clock and *nordestino* expats and fun-loving Cariocas congregate to listen to performances of *forró* and *repentistas* (musical preachers) as well as samba and *música popular Brasileiro* (MPB). To get to the *feira,* take any bus marked São Cristóvão leaving from the Zona Sul. By night, take a taxi.

Lapa

One of Rio's most traditional and notorious neighborhoods, Lapa has had many incarnations. It was originally a beach known as the "Spanish Sands" before being paved over and made into a rather posh 19th-century residential neighborhood. The **Passeio Público** (Rua do Passeio Público, Lapa, 7:30am-9pm daily) evokes what Lapa must have been like when it was still a swank *bairro* where well-to-do families strolled beneath the shady trees of this elegant park.

By the turn of the 20th century, Lapa's fortunes had declined. Until the late 1990s, the neighborhood was very down and out. Then, unexpectedly, a renaissance began to take hold of Lapa, which became famous for its intensely vibrant nightlife, where Cariocas from all walks of life congregate to eat, drink, and dance the night away. Lapa is still somewhat seedy around the edges—take cabs at night. It's still a wonderfully atmospheric slice of old Rio that shouldn't be missed.

ARCOS DA LAPA

Lapa's most iconic landmark is the **Arcos da Lapa** (much of it passes above Largo da Lapa). Originally known as the Aqueduto da Carioca, this distinctly Roman 42-arch aqueduct was built in 1750 to supply fresh water from the Rio da Carioca to the residents of Centro.

CATEDRAL METROPOLITANA

Close to the Arcos de Lapa, the **Catedral Metropolitana** (Av. República de Chile 245, tel. 21/2240-2669, 7am-6pm daily, free) is a cone-shaped modernist cathedral built between 1964 and 1979. The spacious interior is coupled with a pared-down minimalism conducive to contemplation. Visit on a sunny day and be bewitched by the colorful patterns refracted through the four immense stained-glass windows. A small **Museu de Arte Sacra** (R$2) includes objects such as the baptismal fonts used to christen the emperors' offspring and the gold roses Princesa Isabel received from Pope Leo XII after abolishing slavery.

Santa Teresa

In the 19th century, wealthy Cariocas built gracious villas along Santa Teresa's narrow winding streets, with terraces and balconies overlooking the blue waters of the Baía de Guanabara. The views are still alluring—as is the neighborhood, which is why after a long period of decline many artists began to move in during the 1960s and '70s, snatching up the dilapidated villas for a song and transforming them into ateliers and galleries. A second revitalization began to take place in 2005, resulting in the trickling in of boutique hotels and fashionable bistros as well as improved security (surrounded by *favelas,* Santa Teresa has traditionally had a somewhat questionable reputation).

Santa Teresa has gradually evolved into a vibrant community, and many small-scale artistic and musical events take place in "Santa" on a regular basis. Among the most popular is **Portas Abertas** (www.chavemestra.com.br), during which resident artists literally "open doors" to their homes and studios—usually during a weekend in mid-August—so you can view their work (and their often fantastic living spaces).

Until *bonde* (trolley) service resumes, get here via minibus (from Largo da Carioca in Centro) or by taxi, but be forewarned that some cabbies refuse to tackle the steep slopes due to the difficulty of getting a return fare. On foot, the quickest, least-exhausting climbs are via the Escadaria Selarón in Lapa and Rua Cândido Mendes (near the Glória Metrô station) in Glória.

MUSEU CHÁCARA DO CÉU

The **Museu Chácara do Céu** (Rua Murtinho Nobre 93, tel. 21/3970-1126, www.museuscastromaya.com.br, noon-5pm Wed.-Mon., R\$2, free Wed.) is among Rio's loveliest museums. Surrounded by a hilltop garden, the museum is located in a modernist house built in 1957 by Raimundo Castro Maia, a wealthy business magnate whose impressive private collection includes the works of some fine Brazilian masters, such as Alberto da Veiga Guignard, Emiliano Di Cavalcanti, and Cândido Portinari.

Adjacent to the museum is the **Parque das Ruínas** (Rua Murtinho Nobre 169, tel. 21/2215-0621, 8am-8pm Tues.-Sun.), a small but leafy park built around the atmospheric ruins of a palace that belonged to Laurinda Santos Lobo, a wealthy Carioca who was a generous patron of the arts during the early 1900s. Today, its renovated remains house a cultural center that features art exhibits. A small café offers magnificent views.

Glória and Catete

In the mid-19th century, the neighborhoods of Glória and Catete lured Rio's burgeoning upper-middle class, and they remained fashionable addresses until the mid-20th century. Since then, the area has lost some of its luster; however, Catete in particular is quite lively, with lots of local bars and restaurants.

IGREJA NOSSA SENHORA DA GLÓRIA DO OUTEIRO

The *bairro* Glória is named after the dazzling white **Igreja Nossa Senhora da Glória do Outeiro** (Praça Nossa Senhora da Glória, Glória, tel. 21/2557-4600, www.outeirodagloria.org.br, 9am-noon and 1pm-5pm Mon.-Fri., 9am-noon Sat.-Sun., free). This early baroque church, built between 1714 and 1739, is one of the most stunning in Rio and a personal favorite of the Brazilian royal family; many princes and princesses have been baptized here. Visiting involves a steep climb up the Ladeira da Glória or a less-exhausting ride up the restored 1940s funicular (accessed at Rua do Russell 300). If the church is closed, ask for the keys at the **Museu da Imperial Irmandade de Nossa Senhora da Glória** (in the annex of the church on Praça Nossa Senhora da Glória, 9am-5pm Mon.-Fri., 9am-1pm Sat.-Sun., R\$2), a small museum with religious art, ex-votos, and some personal belongings of the Empress Teresa Cristina.

bucolic Santa Teresa

Favelas

The first *favelas* ("slums") in Rio de Janeiro developed in the late 1890s. The federal government had offered land to demobilized soldiers from northeastern Brazil so that they could settle on Rio's vacant slopes. When the government went back on its word, the soldiers occupied the promised land and baptized it Morro da Favela (*favela* is a tough, thorny plant native to the semiarid Northeast). Subsequent *favelados* were freed slaves who immigrated to Rio in search of work and settled on the hillsides. As Rio grew, so did its *favelas*. Today, Rio has more than 600 *favelas*, home to 20-25 percent of the city's population. Unfortunately, they are growing at a much faster rate than the rest of the city.

Rio's *favelas* are notorious for their proximity to Rio's upscale neighborhoods and the drug cartels that control many of them. The drug lords maintain order and security in return for residents' loyalty. Consequences include drug use, drug dealing, and violent shoot-outs between drug lords and the police. While some *favelas* are desolate places where families live in minuscule shacks, others have developed into organized communities that engage in grassroots activism. Residents may have low-paying jobs in surrounding neighborhoods, access to day care, medical clinics, and local businesses, and live in concrete or cinder-block houses with fridges, stoves, TVs, and Wi-Fi.

Over the last two decades, projects such as Favela Bairro have helped integrate these communities into the city's urban fabric. *Favelas* are now included on city maps, and *favelados* are being given legal titles to their property. Rio's government has also installed permanent police units (UPPs) in many of Rio's more centrally located *favelas*.

Favela tours are available with guides such as English-speaking Marcelo Armstrong, who has been operating **Favela Tour** (tel. 21/3322-2727, www.favelatour.com.br) for more than 20 years. He leads groups on three-hour walking tours of the *favelas* of Rocinha and Vila Canoas; part of the tour fee is donated to community projects. Personalized tours are available with **Favela Adventure** (tel. 21/8221-5572, http://favelatour.org), founded by Rocinha native DJ Zezinho. During a customized tour (4-6 hours), visitors are adopted by English-speaking residents as they visit capoeira classes, samba *festas,* and local eateries.

PALÁCIO AND PARQUE DO CATETE

When Brazil was declared a republic, the **Palácio do Catete,** the former mansion of a German baron, became the official residence of Brazil's presidents. It remained so until 1960, when president No. 18, Juscelino Kubitschek, moved the capital to Brasília. Kubitschek was also responsible for transforming his opulent former digs into the **Museu da República** (Rua do Catete 153, Catete, tel. 21/3235-2650, www.museudarepublica.org.br, 10am-4:30pm Tues.-Fri., 11am-5:30pm Sat.-Sun., R$6, free Wed. and Sun.). The highlight is the apartment where President Getúlio Vargas lived—and died. Seemingly frozen in time from the day he shot himself in 1954, it features the smoking revolver along with his bloodied pajamas with the fatal bullet hole. The palace itself, with its stained-glass windows, shiny parquet floors, and lavish marble fixtures, is quite grand.

It is surrounded by the **Parque do Catete** (9am-6pm daily), a green oasis decked out with imperial palms, fish ponds, and serpentine paths. The grounds include an exhibition space, a theater, a small cinema, and a café. Adjacent to the *palácio* is the small **Museu de Folclore Edison Carneiro** (Rua do Catete 179-181, Catete, tel. 21/2285-0441, www.cnfcp.gov.br, 9am-5pm Tues.-Fri., 3pm-6pm Sat.-Sun., free), which has a collection of Brazilian folk art.

Flamengo and Laranjeiras

Stretching along the Baía de Guanabara from Centro to the tunnel that leads to Copacabana is the sprawling *bairro* of Flamengo. In the 19th and early 20th centuries, it was one of Rio's poshest residential neighborhoods. To this day, gracious belle epoque mansions and art deco apartment buildings still line its wide avenues and tree-lined side streets.

Santa Teresa, Glória, Catete, and Flamengo

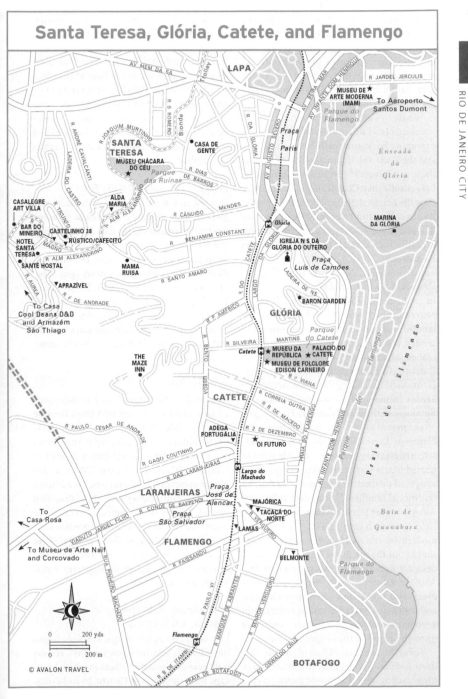

Squeezed between Flamengo, Catete, and Cosme Velho is the equally lovely *bairro* of Laranjeiras, whose name attests to its rural origins, when orchards of "orange trees" reigned. Although there are few sights to be seen, Laranjeiras is one of Rio's most charming neighborhoods.

While you'll glimpse snatches of Flamengo (and adjacent Botafogo) as you're careening back and forth between Centro and the Zona Sul, its worthwhile to wander the area's streets if you have time to spare. Less chaotic than Centro and far less touristy than the Zona Sul, these neighborhoods offer an appealing and colorful slice of Carioca life, and the area shelters one of Rio's most extensive recreational spaces, the Parque do Flamengo.

PARQUE DO FLAMENGO

In 1960, much of Flamengo's beach disappeared beneath tons of earth. This radical landfill was part of an ambitious project to create a vast public park on prime oceanfront real estate that would come to be known as Parque do Flamengo (Av. Infante Dom Henrique). Extending from the Aeroporto Santos Dumont all the way to the Praia de Botafogo, to this day Parque do Flamengo is often referred to as Aterro do Flamengo—the Flamengo Landfill. Spearheading this massive undertaking was a formidable woman named Maria Carlota de Macedo Soares. A vanguard intellectual from one of Rio's most traditional families, "Lota" was the lover of American poet Elizabeth Bishop (who, at the time, lived with Lota in Rio). A great fan of modernism and a self-taught architect, Lota sought out the talents of leading landscape designer Roberto Burle Marx and architect Affonso Eduardo Reidy. Battling bureaucracy and machismo—her all-male crew and colleagues balked at taking orders from a woman—she was able to carry out most (though not all) of the original project.

Today this sweeping ribbon of green is Rio's most popular playground. It contains running, cycling, and skateboard paths, playing fields, a children's park, a puppet theater, and an area reserved for model planes. It is also home to the somber Monumento aos Mortos de Segunda Guerra Mundial, which pays homage to the lives of Brazilian soldiers lost during World War II. On Sundays and holidays, part of Avenida Infante Dom Henrique is closed to traffic, and Cariocas descend on the park in droves. On weekend evenings, outdoor concerts feature top names in Brazilian music.

MUSEU DE ARTE MODERNA

Housed in a stunning modernist steel and glass creation, designed by Affonso Eduardo Reidy and overlooking the Baía de Guanabara, the Museu de Arte Moderna (Av. Infante Dom Henrique 85, Flamengo, tel. 21/2240-4944, www.mamrio.com.br, noon-6pm Tues.-Fri., noon-7pm Sat.-Sun., R$8) boasts one of Brazil's most important collections of 20th-century art. The museum has a cinema, an excellent design shop, a café, and a sleek, pricey restaurant, Laguiole (tel. 21/2517-3129, noon-5pm Mon.-Fri.).

OI FUTURO

Operated by the Brazilian telecommunications giant Oi, Oi Futuro (Rua Dois de Dezembro 63, Flamengo, tel. 21/3131-3060, www.oifuturo.org.br, 11am-8pm Tues.-Sun.) is a cutting-edge cultural center located in a brilliantly renovated early 20th-century phone company headquarters. In addition to a delightful display of vintage Brazilian phones, Oi's rotating temporary exhibits are clearly focused on the future, combining contemporary visual arts with technology. There are also concerts, dance performances, and film screenings, and the rooftop terrace café has terrific views.

Botafogo, Cosme Velho, and Urca

Like neighboring Flamengo, Botafogo began life as bucolic getaway where wealthy Cariocas built seaside weekend palaces in which to escape from the stress of Centro. In its heyday, the white crescent beach of Botafogo was the equivalent of Ipanema today. Although it remains lovely from an aesthetic viewpoint (and serves as a very scenic soccer field), the pollution here means nobody would dream of bathing in its waters these days. The neighborhood has suffered from an onslaught of verticalization via modern high-rises and shopping centers. However, its tranquil, leafy side streets are stuffed with cinemas, bookstores, and restaurants that are prized by Cariocas and largely ignored by tourists.

To the north of Botafogo, Cosme Velho is a pretty residential neighborhood that winds its way up the hills toward Corcovado. At the Estação Cosme Velho, hordes of tourists line up to catch the mini-train that whisks them up the mountain to the outstretched arms of *Cristo Redentor.*

Squeezed onto a promontory facing Botafogo, the tiny residential neighborhood of Urca has resisted much of the urban mayhem characteristic of Rio's other beachside *bairros.* It is a lovely place to stroll around, take in some alluring views, and watch local fisherman cast their lines off into the Baía de Guanabara.

MUSEU DO ÍNDIO

Occupying a handsome 19th-century mansion in Botafogo, the **Museu do Índio** (Rua das Palmeiras 55, Botofago, tel. 21/3214-8700, www.museudoindio.org.br, 9am-5:30pm Tues.-Fri., 1pm-5pm Sat.-Sun., R$3, free Sun.) was founded in 1953 by noted Brazilian anthropologist Darcy Ribeiro. Linked to FUNAI—Brazil's national foundation of indigenous affairs—it possesses an important collection of artifacts reflecting Brazil's diverse native peoples. Among the objects on display are hunting and cooking implements, traditional costumes—including headdresses fashioned out of the Technicolor plumage of Amazonian parrots and toucans—musical instruments, and religious talismans. The museum shop sells an attractive (and decently priced) array of authentic handicrafts.

MORRO DONA MARTA

Rising up from Rua São Clemente, Dona Marta was one of Rio's most infamously dangerous *favelas* before becoming the first to receive a UPP (Police Pacification Unit) in 2008. Shortly thereafter, residents were happy to receive a *plano inclinado* elevator to whisk them up the *morro* to their homes (instead of the 788 precarious stairs cut into the vertiginously steep hillside). Today, visitors can also take the free elevator, which makes five stops on its way to the top. At Estação 3, visit Praça Cantão, where dozens of homes have been painted in juicy fruit hues by Dutch artists Dre Urhann and Jeroen Koolhaus. At the summit, the Mirante Dona Marta offers stunning city and bay views, while the statue of *Cristo Redentor* looms overhead. A short walk through narrow streets leads to the Espaço Michael Jackson, where a lifelike bronze statue and mosaic mural by artist Romero Britto commemorates the spot where MJ filmed the Spike Lee-directed video to his song "They Don't Care About Us."

Free maps are available at the Rio Top Tour kiosk near the entrance to the elevator. If you don't speak Portuguese, take one of themed tours with local resident Thiago Firminio, who runs **Favela Santa Marta Tour** (tel. 21/9177-9459, www.favelasantamartatour. blogspot.com.br, 2 hours, R$50).

CASA DAROS

Rio scored a coup when it was chosen to house the first Latin American outpost by the Swiss Daros Foundation, whose Zurich headquarters consolidates one of the most renowned collections of Latin American art on the planet. **Casa Daros** (Rua General Severiano 159, Botafogo, tel. 21/2275-0246, www.casa-daros.net, noon-8pm Wed.-Sat., noon-6pm Sun., R$12, free Wed.) plays host to temporary exhibits as well as a permanent collection of 117 works by contemporary artists. The Casa alone is worth a visit; the landmark neoclassical house dates to 1866 and originally functioned as an orphanage. The imposing building was designed by Francisco

Joaquim de Bethancourt da Silva, who is also responsible for the Centro Cultural Banco do Brasil. There is a boutique and the wonderful café-restaurant, Mira!, where you can enjoy a meal al fresco beneath a row of elegant imperial palms.

★ CORCOVADO

One of Rio's most instantly recognizable and oft-visited icons, "Hunchback" (the English translation lacks the lyrical sonority of its Portuguese name) Corcovado mountain rises straight up from the center of Rio to a lofty 700 meters (2,300 feet). Equally iconic is the 30-meter (100-foot) art deco statue *Cristo Redentor* (Christ the Redeemer), his outstretched arms enveloping the surrounding city, which crowns Corcovado's sheer granite face. The statue, a gift from France to commemorate 100 years of Brazilian independence in 1921, didn't actually make it up to the top of the mountain until 1931. Since then, however, it has become a true beacon, visible from almost anywhere in the city. It is particularly striking at night when, due to a powerful illumination system, the *Cristo* glows like an otherworldly angel against the darkened sky.

The most scenic way to get to the top of Corcovado is by taking the 19th-century cogwheel train from the **Estação de Ferro do Corcovado** (Rua Cosme Velho 530, Cosme Velho, www.corcovado.com.br, tel. 21/2558-1329, departures every 30 minutes 8:30am-7pm daily, R$46 round-trip), which was inaugurated in 1884 by Dom Pedro II. The crazily steep ride takes 17 minutes—with a stop at Paineiras station—and treats you to stunning views, especially if you're at the back or on the right side of the train. At the top, reach the *Cristo* by walking up a flight of 220 steep steps or taking an escalator or panoramic elevator. From Paineiras station, where there's a parking lot for cars, you can hop a van (make sure it's registered with IBAMA, the parks organization)—round-trip fares cost R$21 (Mon.-Fri.) and R$31 (Sat.-Sun.). It's best to beat the crowds by heading up early on a weekday morning, when you'll have the added privilege of seeing Rio bathed in golden light—be sure to choose a clear day for your visit.

MUSEU INTERNACIONAL DE ARTE NAÏF DO BRASIL

The **Museu Internacional de Arte Naïf do Brasil** (Rua Cosme Velho 561, Cosme Velho, tel. 21/2205-8612, 10am-6pm Tues.-Fri., 10am-5pm Sat.-Sun., R$12) lays claim to having the world's largest collection of *arte naïf,* or naive art. The delightfully expressive and colorful paintings in this colonial mansion portray many elements of popular Brazilian culture, including *futebol,* Carnaval, and scenes from daily life. Although most of the exhibited works, spanning five centuries, are by self-taught Brazilian artists, there are international works from more than 100 countries. A small boutique sells *naïf* art from contemporary artists, and there's also an organic café.

A little farther uphill from the museum, on the opposite side of the street, is the **Largo de**

Cristo Redentor atop Corcovado

Pão de Açúcar

and small shops. The second stop is at the actual 396-meter (1,300-foot) summit of Pão de Açúcar, where you can toast the view with champagne or a beer.

The cars depart for the top every 20 minutes from **Praia Vermelha** (Av. Pasteur 520, Urca, tel. 21/2546-8400, www.bondinho.com.br, 8am-9pm daily, ticket booths close at 7:45pm, R$53 round-trip). Be sure the day is a clear one, but to avoid long lines, steer clear of weekends, holidays, and peak hours (10am-3pm). If you're in a romantic frame of mind—or would like to be—make the trip in the late afternoon. The sunset and twilight, with the lights of Rio glittering in the dusk against the mountain silhouettes, are truly bewitching.

Adventurous types can hike the steep but short trails from Praça General Tibúrcio up to Morro da Urca (and continue by cable car at a reduced rate) or scale Morro Pão de Açúcar in the company of a climbing outfit. The 2.4-km (1.5-mi) Pista Claudio Coutinho is an easier, paved trail that winds its way along the sea-lapped base of both *morros*.

Copacabana and Leme

Although its glamour days are long gone, Copacabana still manages to live up to its legend as the world's most famous strip of white sand. Originally a tiny fishing village, with the construction of the luxurious Copacabana Palace hotel in 1923, the wealthy and fabulous came flocking. A slew of streamlined art deco apartment buildings soon rose up along the beachfront's Avenida Atlântica. Before long, "Copa" was not just *the* place to live but *the* place to party. Tycoons, movie stars, royalty, and the international jet set transformed its sweeping carpet of sand into their personal playground.

While many of Rio's rich and fashionable have since moved on to the more chic neighborhoods of Ipanema and Leblon, Copa has become—for better or for worse—one of Rio's most eclectic, vibrant, and democratic neighborhoods, a place where street kids and millionaires, models and muscle men, doormen and nannies from the Northeast of

Boticário (Rua Cosme Velho 822). Named after the imperial family's *boticário* (apothecary), who was a resident, this enchanting 19th-century square resembles a period film set, with colorfully painted villas offset by tropical foliage.

★ PÃO DE AÇÚCAR

The monumental chunk of granite guarding the entrance to the Baía de Guanabara is known as **Pão de Açúcar.** Rio's original Tupi inhabitants referred to it as *pau-nh-acugua* (high, pointed, mountain). When the Portuguese arrived on the scene, both the Tupi term and the mountain reminded them of a *pão de açúcar* (sugar loaf), a conical mound of sugar made by pouring liquid cane juice into a rounded mold. The name stuck.

Reach the summit by taking a glass-sided **cable car** up the mountain—an unforgettably scenic journey offering panoramic views of Rio and the Baía de Guanabara. The first stop is at **Morro da Urca,** a 210-meter (690-foot) mountain, where there is a restaurant

Beach Dos and Don'ts

Cariocas have developed a very sophisticated *cultura de praia* with habits and codes worth taking note of if you want to blend in.

- **Don't** wear a bathing suit from home; purchase one on location. Rio's cutting-edge bikini and *sunga* (the male version of a bikini) styles are light-years ahead of the rest of the world, and prices are generally affordable.

- **Do** wear flip-flops (Havaianas are the coolest) to and from the beach and **don't** wear shoes.

- **Don't** take any valuables to the beach and don't leave possessions unguarded. Take a beach bag instead of a purse and ask a respectable-looking neighbor to keep an eye on your stuff while you take a dip.

- **Don't** bring a towel to the beach. *Cangas* are lighter, de rigueur, and are sold all over the beaches. For more comfort, rent a chair.

- **Don't** schlep food or drinks to the beach. Rio's beaches are well-serviced with food and drink vendors.

- **Don't** go swimming if a red flag is flying; Rio's beaches have strong currents in places. Only go in the water where locals are already swimming.

- **Don't** get a sunburn. Not only will you suffer on your vacation, but the red lobster look will brand you a foolish gringo.

If you're female:

- **Do** know that Cariocas are not shy about revealing a lot of flesh. However…

- **Don't** take your top off. Topless sunbathing is a no-no and Cariocas are very proud of their tan lines.

- **Do** cover up (lightly) with a lightweight top and microshorts or skirts when walking to/from the beach.

If you're male:

- **Don't** don a Speedo-style bathing suit. Stylish *sungas* are modeled on men's full briefs.

- **Do** know that surfing shorts are for surfing or wearing over your bathing suit, *not* for lounging around on the sand or swimming.

- **Do** flaunt your bare chest to/from the beach, but otherwise wear a T-shirt.

Brazil, and American tourists from the deepest Midwest all rub shoulders. During the day senior citizens swarm the beaches and the dozens of bakeries along the main drag of Avenida Nossa Senhora de Copacabana, but by night the stretch of Avenida Atlântica toward Ipanema is a hot spot for prostitutes and for the (many foreign) johns who travel to Copa in search of more piquant forms of R&R. Inland from the ocean, unpretentious neighborhood restaurants, *botecos,* and street markets coexist alongside 24-hour gyms and juice bars. Copa may be a little seedy in places, but it is also fun—and whatever you may think of the *bairro,* there is no denying the allure of its beach.

★ COPACABANA BEACH

Urban beaches don't get any more dazzling than this 4.5-kilometer (2.8-mi) strip that stretches in a gorgeous arc from Pão de Açúcar to the Forte de Copacabana. The sand is sugary fine and white, and a striking contrast to the blue of the open Atlantic and the hypnotically wavy, white-and-black mosaic promenade that separates it from busy Avenida Atlântica. From dawn to dusk there is always something happening on Copa's beach—whether it's a sunrise yoga class for seniors, a *Vogue* photo shoot, or an early evening volleyball practice for preteen girls. You can get a tan or a tattoo, drink a caipirinha at a fancy *barraca* or an icy *água de coco* sold by one of many hundreds of *ambulantes,* who hawk everything from strangely addictive bags of Globo *biscoitos* to transistor radios. Of course, in a pinch, you can go swimming—the chilly temperatures coupled with an undercurrent demand caution—but you can also do so much more.

Like the neighborhood itself, Copacabana beach is stratified, with different points occupied by different "tribes." The 1-kilometer (0.6-mi) stretch closest to the Túnel Novo that leads to Botafogo—between Morro do Leme and Avenida Princesa Isabel—is known as **Praia do Leme** (the small, attractive residential *bairro* behind it is also known as Leme). Leme's warm waters are popular with families and older residents, while its swells lure surfers. A short path around the base of Pedra do Leme offers great views, or head to the nearby army base and follow a 20-minute paved trail that winds through a hummingbird-filled Atlantic forest to the summit, which is guarded by the whitewashed 18th-century **Forte Duque de Caxias** (Praça Almirante Júlio de Noronha, Leme, tel. 21/3223-5076, www.cep.ensino.eb.br, 9:30am-4:30pm Tues.-Sun., R$4).

The stretch of Copacabana in front of the Copacabana Palace is a gay haunt, while the patch near Rua Santa Clara is popular with fans of *futebol* and *futevolei* (a Brazilian version of volleyball). Closer to Ipanema, Postos 5 and 6 (posto refers to the beacon-like lifeguard posts) draw an eclectic mix of seniors and *favela* kids. At the very end, in front of the Forte de Copacabana, is one of the oldest and most traditional fishermen's colonies in Rio.

★ Ipanema and Leblon

The most coveted—and expensive—slice of beachfront property in Rio de Janeiro is the area from which the first chords of "A Garota de Ipanema" ("The Girl from Ipanema") were set down by two poets. The year was 1962, and Tom Jobim and Vinicius de Moraes were at their favorite neighborhood bar when an enticingly bronzed young Carioca sashayed by on her way to the beach, inspiring the languorously cool bossa nova jewel.

Copacabana beach

Botafogo, Leme, and Copacabana

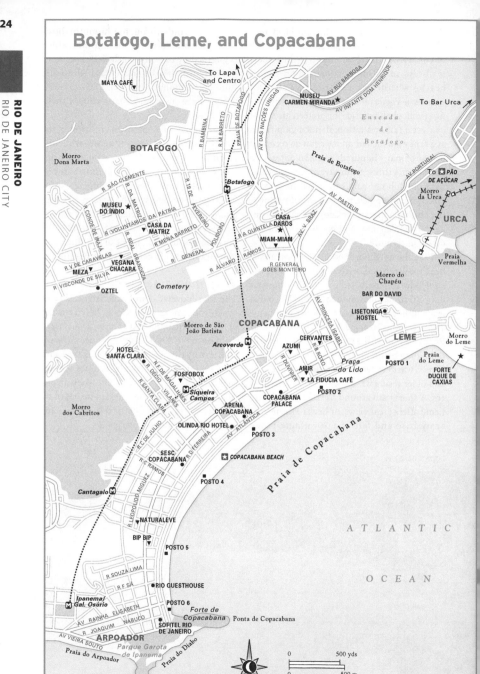

MAYA CAFÉ

To Lapa
and Centro

MUSEU
CARMEN MIRANDA

To Bar Urca

AV RUI BARBOSA
AV INFANTE DOM HENRIQUE

Enseada
de
Botafogo

R BAMBINA
R M BARRETO
PRAIA DE BOTAFOGO
AV DAS NAÇÕES UNIDAS

BOTAFOGO

Morro
Dona Marta

Praia de Botafogo

To PÃO
DE AÇÚCAR

AV PORTUGAL

R SÃO CLEMENTE
Botafogo

Morro
da Urca

R 19 DE FEVEREIRO

AV PASTEUR

URCA

MUSEU
DO ÍNDIO

R DA MATRIZ
R DA PÁTRIA
CASA
DAROS

Praia
Vermelha

R CONDE DE IRAJÁ
R VOLUNTÁRIOS
R REAL GRANDEZA

CASA DA
MATRIZ

R A QUINTELA BRAZ

R MENA BARRETO

MIAM-MIAM

AV V. BRAZ

R V DE CARAVELAS

R GENERAL

R ÁLVARO RAMOS

VEGANA
CHÁCARA

R GENERAL
GÓES MONTEIRO

Morro do
Chapéu

MEZA

R VISCONDE DE SILVA

BAR DO DAVID

OZTEL

Cemetery

LISETONGA
HOSTEL

AV PRINCESA ISABEL

Morro de São
João Batista

COPACABANA

CERVANTES

LEME

Morro
do Leme

Arcoverde

AZUMI

R B. ROXO

R DJVIVIER

Praia
do Leme

HOTEL
SANTA CLARA

R F DE MAGALHÃES

FOSFOBOX

AMIR

Praça
do Lido

POSTO 1

FORTE
DUQUE DE
CAXIAS

R DÉCIO VILARES

R SANTA CLARA

Siqueira
Campos

LA FIDUCIA CAFÉ

POSTO 2

Morro
dos Cabritos

ARENA
COPACABANA

COPACABANA
PALACE

R C DE JULHO

OLINDA RIO HOTEL

AV ATLÂNTICA

POSTO 3

R D FERREIRA

SESC
COPACABANA

COPACABANA BEACH

R C RAMOS

R LEOPOLDO MIGUEZ

POSTO 4

Praia de Copacabana

Cantagalo

ATLANTIC

NATURALEVE

BIP BIP

POSTO 5

OCEAN

R SOUZA LIMA

R F SÁ

RIO GUESTHOUSE

Ipanema/
Gal. Osório

POSTO 6

Forte de
Copacabana

Ponta de Copacabana

AV RAINHA ELISABETH

R JOAQUIM NABUCO

SOFITEL RIO
DE JANEIRO

AV VIEIRA SOUTO

ARPOADOR

Parque Garota
de Ipanema

Praia do Diabo

Praia do Arpoador

0   500 yds

0   500 m

© AVALON TRAVEL

Ipanema beach

Since then, Ipanema has been a magnet for a cosmopolitan mix of artists, musicians, and leftist intellectuals, along with a rich and trendy crowd who consistently fall prey to its tree-lined streets, fashionable bars and boutiques, and magnificent white sands. Ipanema retains a more bohemian edge than neighboring Leblon, which is slightly more sedate and residential (and richer), but no less appealing. Both, however, carry off the impressive feat of being both incredibly chic and disarmingly casual. To wit: The sight of tattooed surfer boys carrying their boards past the discreetly jeweled millionaires ensconced at the terraces of five-star restaurants is extremely common.

Ipanema and Leblon are essentially one long and captivating beach divided by the narrow Jardim de Alah canal. Straighter and narrower than Copacabana, this beach is no less scenic—Ipanema begins at the **Pedra do Arpoador,** a dramatic rock jutting into the sea, and Leblon ends at the twin-headed **Morro de Dois Irmãos,** a fantastically shaped mountain that really does conjure up

the heads of "Two Brothers." During the week, the beaches are tranquil, but when the weekend rolls around, the sand is a sea of bikinied and *sunga*-ed bodies, engaging in activities as varied as playing *futevolei* and smoking illicit joints. On Sundays, the main oceanfront drags of Avenida Viera Souto (Ipanema) and Avenida Delfim Moreira (Leblon) are closed to traffic, and the whole area becomes a massive outdoor recreational scene.

Like Copa, Ipanema and Leblon are divided into tribal territories. With its big waves, **Praia do Arpoador** (the edge of Ipanema closest to Copa) is a mecca for surfers. The area around **Posto 8** (off Rua Farme de Amoedo) is a magnet for gay men to show off their *sungas*, while **Posto 9** (the area off of Rua Vinicius de Moraes) has long been the territory of artists and intellectuals who would rather flaunt their leftist viewpoints. **Posto 10** is pretty much a family affair, where young couples congregate with their tots to take advantage of the playground and diaper-changing facilities.

Lagoa

When strolling along the shady streets of Ipanema and Leblon, you'll see a vast lagoon ringed by luxury villas and apartment buildings set against the backdrop of mountains, including Corcovado. The **Lagoa Rodrigo de Freitas**—or simply Lagoa—is a saltwater lagoon of posh private clubs, skating parks, tennis courts, and a heliport where already svelte Cariocas power-walk, jog, and cycle until they break a sweat. The less athletically inclined prefer to sip an *água de coco* or a caipirinha at one of the many kiosks around the lagoon; all serve food and drinks. In the evening, live music is often played at the kiosks (the best are near the Parque dos Patins and the Corte do Cangalo).

On the north side of the Lagoa, the lower reaches of **Parque da Catacumba** (Av. Epitácio Pessoa 300, Lagoa, tel. 21/2247-9949, 8am-5pm, Tues.-Sun.) consist of winding paths through jungly gardens, a vivid backdrop for 31 sculptures created by Brazilian

Ipanema, Leblon, and Lagoa

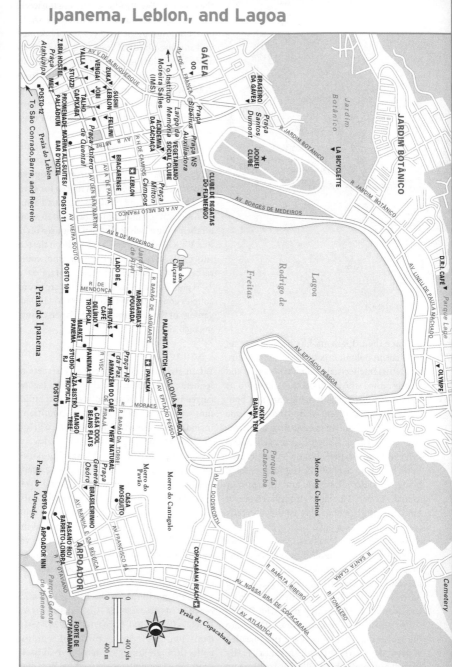

and international artists. A steep but easy 20-minute trail leads through replanted Atlantic rain forest to lookout points that offer sublime views of the entire Zona Sul. The park's name stems from the belief that the site originally sheltered "catacombs" for Rio's original Tamoio inhabitants.

Jardim Botânico

On the far side of the Lagoa (across from Ipanema) is the lush upscale neighborhood of Jardim Botânico. Some of the city's chicest restaurants and bars are tucked away here.

A 138-hectare (340-acre) urban oasis, the **Jardim Botânico** itself (Rua Jardim Botânico 1008, tel. 21/3874-1808, www.jbrj.gov.br, 8am-5pm daily, R$7) offers an unparalleled mix of native Atlantic forest, lagoons covered with giant lily pads, and more than 8,000 plant species. Many of them—pineapples, cinnamon, and tea among them—were introduced here prior to their cultivation in the rest of Brazil. Highlights include the scent garden, the cactus garden, and the fabulous *orquidário,* featuring more than 1,000 species of wild orchids. Kids (and adults) with a fondness for the mildly gruesome will enjoy the carnivorous plant collection.

Adjacent to the Jardim Botânico is the **Parque Lage** (Rua Jardim Botânico 414, tel. 21/3257-1800, 8am-5pm daily, free), designed by 19th-century English landscaper John Tyndale. Its winding paths snake around small ponds, grottos, an aquarium, and through the lush tropical landscape that covers the lower slopes of Corcovado (a steep trail winds up through the **Parque Nacional da Tijuca**). In the midst of the greenery is the early 20th-century mansion of a wealthy industrialist who built the stately abode for his opera singer wife. The internal courtyard is home to **D.R.I. Café** (Rua Jardim Botânico 414, tel. 21/2226-8125, www.driculinaria.com.br, 9am-5pm daily), a beguiling spot for coffee. The palace houses the Escola de Artes Visuais, an art school where temporary exhibits are often held.

Gávea

Less hip and happening than Ipanema and neighboring Leblon, Gávea is still an attractive neighborhood with lots of leafy streets, easy access to the Lagoa, and a lively bar scene.

JOQUEI CLUBE

You've likely never seen a racetrack with such stupendous surroundings (the *Cristo Redentor* hovers directly above the bleachers). Built in 1926, Rio's Joquei Clube, also known as the **Hipódromo da Gávea** (Praça Santos Dumont 131, tel. 21/3534-9000, www.jcb.com.br) was featured in a scene in the 1946 Hitchcock film *Notorious,* during which Cary Grant and Ingrid Bergman take some time out from espionage and romance to bet on the horses. Even if you don't want to gamble (race times are 6:15pm Mon., 5pm Fri., 2:45pm Sat.-Sun.), the club is a fun place to grab a drink (no shorts allowed) or to indulge in a relaxing massage or treatment at **Nirvana** (tel. 21/2187-0100, www.enirvana.com.br), an airy spa that offers yoga and Pilates.

INSTITUTO MOREIRA SALLES

Located halfway up a steep hill full of striking villas, the **Instituto Moreira Salles** (IMS; Rua Marquês de São Vicente 476, tel. 21/3284-7400, www.ims.com.br, 11am-8pm Tues.-Sun., free) is one of the city's loveliest cultural centers. One of Rio's most prominent families, the Moreira Salles (owners of Unibanco, a major bank) commissioned architect Olavo Redig de Campos to build this house in 1951, and the result is Brazilian modernism at its most streamlined and alluring. The equally enticing gardens were landscaped by Roberto Burle Marx. The Moreira Salles family has always had a strong commitment to the arts (Walter Salles Jr., director of the films *Central Station* and *The Motorcycle Diaries,* is a member of the clan), and part of their important collection of historical photographs, many depicting 19th- and 20th-century Rio de Janeiro, can be viewed, along with temporary exhibitions. There is also a cinema, boutique, and a café that serves a lavish afternoon tea and breakfasts on weekends.

São Conrado, Barra, and Recreio

Rio's coastal road, Avenida Niemeyer, goes through a long tunnel that burrows beneath the Morro de Dois Irmãos, whose slopes are home to one of Rio's largest *favelas,* Vidigal. While their beaches are attractive, the neighborhoods here lack the history and charm of the Zona Sul, and none were laid out with pedestrians in mind—cars rule, but the coastline is also well served by buses from the Zona Sul, with destinations marked Barra and Recreio.

São Conrado is a small neighborhood full of luxury high-rise condominiums and a fancy shopping mall. In a startling contrast, these posh edifices gaze directly onto Rio's biggest and most notorious *favela:* Rocinha, home to more than 200,000 residents, whose brick and cement dwellings cover the otherwise rain forest-carpeted Morro de Dois Irmãos. Although Rio is all about glaring contradictions and brutal extremes, nowhere else is the divide between rich and poor so prominently, fascinatingly, and perversely apparent. São Conrado's main draw is the small and spectacular Praia do Pepino (Cucumber Beach), where hang gliders burn off their adrenaline after taking off from the neighboring peaks of Pedra da Gávea and Pedra Bonita.

Another long tunnel brings you to the developed, suburban, Miami-like *bairro* of Barra da Tijuca, known simply as Barra. Two decades ago, this 16-kilometer (10-mi) stretch of coastline was little more than a long, wild sweep of white sand with a few *barracas.* Barra's saving grace is its beach, which remains amazingly unspoiled, particularly during the week. The trendiest strip, at the beginning of the Barra between Postos 1 and 2, is known as Praia do Pepê (access from Av. do Pepê). Although the surf is rough, you can swim here.

Barra da Tijuca turns into the 11-kilometer (7-mi) long beach known as Recreio dos Bandeirantes, whose rough waves are a magnet for Rio's surfing crowd. Particularly attractive is the small and secluded Prainha beach, at the end of Recreio. The spectacular waves and presence of several renowned surfing academies make it a mecca for surfers. Even more deserted is Grumari, whose reddish sands are framed by spectacular mountains covered in lush native Atlantic forest. Both Prainha and Grumari are located in protected nature reserves. Despite the fact they can't be reached by bus, they can fill up on the weekends with Cariocas seeking a quick back-to-nature fix. Near Grumari, Praia de Abricó is Rio's only nude beach.

MUSEU CASA DO PONTAL

Inland from the far end of Recreio dos Bandeirantes is the Museu Casa do Pontal (Estrada do Pontal 3295, tel. 21/2490-3278, www.popular.art.br/museucasadopontal, 9:30am-5pm Tues.-Sun., R$10). Back in the late 1940s, French designer and art collector Jacques Van de Beuque began traveling throughout Brazil (especially the Northeast), where he discovered a fantastically rich artisanal tradition that nobody—not even Brazilians—was aware of. To preserve and promote these works, he built a vast house surrounded by tranquil gardens. Today, it shelters the largest collection of Brazilian folk art in the country, with more than 5,000 works ranging from wonderful clay figures of popular Northeast folk heroes to the extravagant costumes worn by celebrants of traditional Bumba-Meu-Boi *festas.* To get here by bus from the Zona Sul, take any bus going to Barra da Tijuca and get off at Barra Shopping to transfer to the 703 or S-20 bus going to Recreio, which will let you off in front of the museum's entrance. Although it takes well over an hour to get here, the final destination is worth it.

SÍTIO ROBERTO BURLE MARX

The idyllic Sítio Roberto Burle Marx (Estrada Roberto Burle Marx 2019, tel. 21/2410-1412, www.sitioburlemarx.blogspot. com, tours by appointment only 9:30am and

1:30pm Tues.-Sun., R$10) is another attraction worth the time and effort to get to. Between 1949 and 1994, this bucolic country estate was the primary residence of renowned landscape architect Roberto Burle Marx, whose most famous projects in Rio include the Parque do Flamengo and Copacabana's iconic black-and-white mosaic "wave" promenade. The colonial house (originally part of a coffee plantation) and adjoining atelier have been transformed into a museum where you can admire the artist's works, possessions, and rich collection of Brazilian folk art. The surrounding nursery and gardens—featuring more than 3,500 plant species collected from Brazil and around the world—were designed with great flair. Indeed, it was said about Marx—who was also a painter—that he used plants as other artists used paint. If you don't have a car, take the bus marked Marambaia-Passeio (No. 387) that passes through the Zona Sul.

ENTERTAINMENT AND EVENTS

Rio boasts a dynamic arts scene. For information (in Portuguese), check out the arts sections of the two daily papers, *Jornal do Brasil* and *O Globo*, or purchase *Veja Rio*, which comes with *Veja* magazine and offers comprehensive listings of everything going on in the city. For upcoming events in English as well as Portuguese, visit www.rioguiaoficial.com.br. *Time Out*'s online English guide to Rio (www.timeout.com.br/rio-de-janeiro/en) is another great source, as is the weekly newspaper *The Rio Times* (www.riotimesonline.com).

★ Carnaval

Why is it that whenever people hear the word *Carnaval,* Rio de Janeiro automatically springs to mind? Rio isn't the only city to host this bacchanalian celebration, but its signature parades, balls, and *escolas de sambas* combined with nonstop merrymaking have made it the most spectacular of Brazil's Carnavals. To experience Rio's hedonistic five-day *festa* in all its butt-swaying, ear-blasting, eye-popping, mind-blowing glory,

make sure to book your accommodations *far* in advance.

DESFILES DAS ESCOLAS

The **Desfiles das Escolas de Samba** is the most famous Carnaval event. It consists of the *desfiles* (parades) of the top *escolas de samba* (known as the Grupo Especial, or Special Group). These take place in a massive concrete stadium called the **Sambódromo** (Rua Marquês de Sapucaí, Praça Onze, Cidade Nova). Designed by Oscar Niemeyer, it can seat 78,000 people. *Desfiles* are held on the Sunday and Monday nights of Carnaval and involve 12 *escolas de samba* that compete against each other.

Each night, six *escolas* have 80 minutes to strut their stuff for a table of judges, who award points for various aspects of their performances, among them choreography, costumes, floats, decorations, *samba de enredo* (theme song), and percussion. Every year, the *escolas* invest incredible amounts of money, time, hard work, and talent in an attempt to outdo one another and be crowned champion. If you miss the competition itself, on the following Saturday you can catch the top schools performing in the championship parade, which also takes place at the Sambódromo. Tickets to this "best of" compilation event are much cheaper than those for the *desfiles.*

Getting cheap **tickets** to the Sambódromo is a tricky affair. Most are purchased long before the event itself—they usually go on sale in January—within minutes of going on sale. Savvy scalpers and travel agents often snatch up the best seats. Two good sources of information are **Rio Services Carnival** (www.rio-carnival.net), which sells tickets online via PayPal, and **Riotur** (www.rioguiaoficial.com.br), the municipal tourist secretariat. The latter sells expensive tickets (R$990-1,600) in private boxes for tourists, which are much more comfortable than the regular concrete bleachers. Tickets for other sections range R$130-600. Try to sit in the central sections (Sections 5, 7, and 9), which offer the best views and the most animation. You can also

Off-Season Carnaval Activities

If you can't get to Rio for Carnaval, you can still experience an authentic slice of the action by taking part in the *ensaios* (rehearsals) every weekend by Rio's various *escolas de samba*. Get a behind-the-scenes glimpse at the makings of a successful *desfile* (parade) and soak up some authentic neighborhood atmosphere, all while listening to terrific samba. Since most schools are in the Zona Norte, sometimes close to *favelas*, take a tour or taxi. The Mangueira and Salgueiro samba schools are the most popular for tourists and are also closest to the Centro.

- **Beija Flor** (Prainha Wallace Paes Leme 1025, Nilópolis, tel. 21/2791-2866, www.beija-flor.com.br)
- **Grande Rio** (Rua Almirante Barroso 5-6, Duque de Caixias, tel. 21/2671-3585, www.academicos-dogranderio.com.br)
- **Império Serrano** (Av. Ministro Edgar Romero 114, Madureira, tel. 21/2489-8722, www.imperioserrano.com)
- **Mangueira** (Rua Visconde de Niterói 1072, Mangueira, tel. 21/3872-6878, www.mangueira.com.br)
- **Portela** (Rua Clara Nunes 81, Madureira, tel. 21/2489-6440, www.gresportela.com.br)
- **Salgueiro** (Rua Silva Teles 104, Andaraí, tel. 21/2238-9226, www.salgueiro.com.br)
- **Unidos da Tijuca** (Clube dos Portuários, Rua Francisco Bicalho 47, Cidade Nova, tel. 21/2263-9679, www.unidosdatijuca.com.br)

As Carnaval approaches, the *escolas de samba* hold dress rehearsals at the Sambódromo, which are open to the public. You can also catch them at the **Cidade do Samba** (Rua Rivadávia Correia 60, Gamboa, tel. 24/2213-2503, www.cidadedosambarj.globo.com, 10am-5pm Tues.-Sat., R$5), a vast complex created out of Rio's abandoned dockside warehouses. Here the *Grupo Especial escolas* have ample space to store materials, sew costumes, build allegorical floats, and display their talents to the public (usually Thurs. nights, when a combined show and buffet costs a whopping R$190). Make sure you take a taxi here.

For more information about *escolas de samba* and *ensaios*, contact the **Liga das Escolas de Samba** (tel. 21/3213-5151, www.liesa.globo.com).

purchase tickets online (make sure the agency is reputable) or in person at Rio travel agencies, which usually charge a commission. If you find yourself without tickets at the last minute, head straight for the Sambódromo and look around for scalpers; they'll be looking around for you. If you're willing to miss the first couple of schools and arrive fashionably late (like most Cariocas), you can usually get some good bargains—make sure you get a plastic card with a magnetic strip, accompanied by a paper ticket with a seat and the *correct* date.

Although you can get to the Sambódromo by bus, these are usually packed, rowdy, and full of pickpockets. You're better off taking a taxi or the Metrô (which runs 24 hours during Carnaval) to Praça Onze (if you're seated in an even-numbered sector) or Central (for an odd-numbered sector).

STREET CARNAVAL

More than 300 neighborhood and resident association *blocos* and *bandas* traditionally take to the streets and let loose in an explosion of music and merrymaking that many swear is way more fun than sitting around in the Sambódromo. Although the costumes of the *blocos* aren't as ornate as those of the *escolas de samba,* some are highly inventive and downright hilarious. Many men—both gay and straight—dress in drag. To join in the fun, all you have to do is appear at a *bloco*'s headquarters on the day and time of its parades (Riotur provides this info). Check to see if you're expected to don the *bloco*'s traditional colors or to purchase a T-shirt (sold on the spot). Festivities usually kick off in the afternoon and last far into the night; for times and dates, pick up a free *Carnaval de Rua* guide published by Riotur or check out their site for online schedules.

BLOCOS AND BANDAS

Centro is home to some of the city's most traditional *blocos*. Among the most popular are **Bafo de Onça, Bloco Cacique de Ramos,** and **Cordão do Bola Preta,** whose followers sport lots of *bolas pretas* (black polka dots). Santa Teresa features the **Carmelitas de Santa Teresa,** Glória has the **Banda da Glória,** and Botafogo boasts several lively traditional *blocos,* among them **Barbas, Bloco de Segunda,** and **Dois Pra Lá, Dois Prá Cá.** Copa's most famous *bloco* is **Bip Bip,** many of whose members are professional musicians, while bohemian Ipanema has some of the most wildly alternative groups, among them **Banda Ipanema, Símpatia É Quase Amor,** and the **Banda Carmen Miranda,** in which men of all sexual orientations don platform shoes and tutti-frutti turbans to pay their respects to the Brazilian Bombshell.

Other outdoor shows and festivities fill the city. Thousands flock to the municipal bash held outside the Sambódromo at **Terreirão do Samba,** as well as the popular **Baile da Cinelândia** and the alternative **Rio Folia,** held beneath the Arcos da Lapa.

CARNAVAL BALLS

The extravagant Carnaval balls of yesteryear are alive and well at Rio's clubs and hotels. Live samba bands supply the rhythms, and costumes—many of them quite spectacular—are de rigueur. Despite air-conditioning, the atmosphere is guaranteed to get hot and steamy as the night wears on. The most famous and fabulous event (costumes or formal wear required) is the **Magic Ball** held at the Copacabana Palace (Av. Atlântica 1702, Copacabana, tel. 21/2445-8790) on Saturday night, which attracts an international throng of rich and gorgeous people for whom R$2,000 (for standing room) is chump change. Tickets to most other balls, however, are in a much more affordable range (R$40-160). The gay-friendly thematic bashes held at Cinelândia's **Scala** club (Av Treze de Maio 23, Centro, tel. 21/2239-4448, www.scalario.com.br) every night during Carnaval are some of the wildest and most spectacular, culminating on the last night with the immensely popular **Gala Gay.** Many other clubs also organize *bailes* in which gay men go all out in terms of cross dressing. Since the one thing Cariocas don't take lightly is Carnaval, no matter where you go, you'll be expected to show up in a seriously extravagant costume.

Réveillon

Ringing in the New Year on **Copacabana Beach** ranks among the most magical and mystical New Year experiences. As night falls, millions of people clad in white congregate on the sands of Copacabana. The white symbolizes the purity of the new year and is also the color associated with Iemanjá, a popular Afro-Brazilian religious deity (*orixá*) whose title is Queen of the Seas. Revelers arrive at the beach bearing her favorite gifts: roses, perfumes, jewelry, and champagne. At the stroke of midnight, they wade into the ocean and toss their offerings into the dark Atlantic. If Iemanjá accepts their gifts, they are ensured a happy year. If the waves sweep them back to shore, better luck next time.

Midnight also signals the start of a gigantic fireworks display and a series of open-air live music shows. Then it's dancing and drinking the night away under the stars until morning, when everyone rings in the first day of the year (and rinses off the night's excesses) with a dip in the ocean.

Performing Arts

Rio's most prestigious performing arts space is the **Theatro Municipal** (Praça Floriano,

Centro, tel. 21/2332-9134, www.theatromunicipal.rj.gov.br), which hosts the biggest national and international names in music, dance, opera, and theater. It also has its own renowned symphony orchestra, opera company, and ballet troupe.

Located inside the grandiose neoclassical former headquarters of the Banco do Brasil, the **Centro Cultural Banco do Brasil** (CCBB; Rua 1 de Março 66, Centro, tel. 21/3808-2000, 9am-9pm Tues.-Sun., www.culturabancodobrasil.com.br/portal) offers a consistently excellent selection of some of Rio's—and Brazil's—finest contemporary theater, dance, film, and music. Many events are free. Banco do Brasil is a major patron of the arts, and the CCBB's magnificent interior welcomes most major national and international art exhibits as well as musical and theatrical performances that travel to and throughout Brazil. With a bookstore and café, it is also a favorite meeting point for Cariocas.

The **Espaço Cultural dos Correios** (Rua Visconde de Itaboraí 20, Centro, tel. 21/2253-1580, www.correios.com.br, noon-7pm Tues.-Sun.) has a great café that overlooks the adjacent Praça dos Correios, where live musical performances frequently take place. On the same street, the **Casa França-Brasil** (Rua Visconde de Itaboraí 78, Centro, tel. 21/2332-5120, www.fcfb.rj.gov.br, 10am-8pm Tues.-Sun.) hosts temporary art exhibits.

One of Rio's oldest and most distinguished theaters, **Teatro João Caetano** (Praça Tiradentes, Centro, tel. 21/2332-9166) features a diverse range of musical and dance as well as theatrical performances. **Fundição Progresso** (Rua dos Arcos 24, Lapa, tel. 21/2220-5070, www.fundicaoprogresso.com.br) is a cleverly renovated historic foundry that operates as a multifaceted performance space. On any given day, you might hear legendary *sambistas,* internationally acclaimed indie rockers, or the Petrobras Symphony Orchestra. It's home to the Intrépida Troupe, a performance group whose works fuse theater, dance, and circus.

The concrete behemoth known as the **Cidade das Artes** (Av. das Américas 5300, Barra da Tijuca, tel. 21/3325-0102, www.cidadedasartes.org) is responsible for bringing a much-needed shot of high culture to the Zona Ouest. Designed by French architect Christian de Portzarparc, it is the largest cultural center in Latin America, possessing state-of-the-art concert spaces, theaters, and cinemas.

Concert Halls
Rio's biggest concert hall is the gigantic, state-of-the-art **Citibank Hall** (Av. Ayrton Senna 3000, Shopping Via Parque, Barra da Tijuca, tel. 11/4003-5588, www.citibankhall.com.br), where major national and international musical, theatrical, and dance events take place. Located beneath the Arcos de Lapa, **Circo Voador** (Rua dos Arcos, Lapa, tel. 21/2533-0354, www.circovoador.com.br) has been one of the city's vanguard outdoor musical venues since the 1980s. The "Flying Circus" continues to host big national stars as well as alternative local bands and theatrical groups. Adjacent to the Museu de Arte Moderno, **Viva Rio** (Av. Infante Dom Henrique 85, Parque do Flamengo, tel. 21/2272-2900, www.vivario.com.br) boasts a humungous concert hall where a diverse sampling of homegrown and imported musical talents are savored against the backdrop of Guanabara Bay. The Carmen-inspired **Miranda** (Av. Borges de Medeiros 1424, Lagoa, tel. 21/2239-0305, www.mirandabrasil.com.br), located in the Lagoon entertainment complex, is a swanky and vaguely retro supper club hosting a diverse range of Brazilian musical and performing artists.

Cinema
Rio is one of Latin America's most important film markets, and you can see everything from Hollywood blockbusters to national, European, independent, and art films. One of the city's biggest cinephile hangouts is the **Espaço Itaú de Cinema** (Praia de Botafogo 316, Botafogo, tel. 21/2559-8750, www.itaucinemas.com.br), with six state-of-the-art screens, a cool bar, and a great bookstore. Nearby are the **Estação Rio**

(Rua Voluntários da Pátria 35, Botafogo, tel. 21/2266-9955) and the **Estação Botafogo** (Rua Voluntários da Pátria 88, Botafogo, tel. 21/2226-1988), which show a mixture of national and international films.

Although Rio was once home to an impressive number of glamorous movie palaces, there are now just two survivors that still screen films. The **Cine Odeon Petrobras** (Praça Mahatma Gandhi 5, Centro, tel. 21/2240-1093, www.grupoestacao.com.br) is a handsomely restored art deco gem in Cinelândia that often hosts star-studded premieres, and the **Roxy** (Av. Nossa Senhora de Copacabana 945-A, Copacabana, tel. 21/2461-2461, www.kinoplex.com.br) is an art deco theater inaugurated in 1938 that has it all: a sweeping staircase, plush lobby, and three large-screen theaters. Far more modern, the **Cinépolis Lagoon** (Av. Borges de Medeiros 1424, Lagoa, tel. 21/3029-2544, www.cinepolis.com.br) is a multiplex whose terrace bar offers incomparable views of the Lagoa and Corcovado.

In late September-early October, it's worth checking out the **Festival do Rio** (www.festivaldorio.com.br), an outstanding international film festival.

NIGHTLIFE

As laid-back and relaxing as Rio can be by day, at night it becomes a buzzing hive of activity. Rio is one of the most musical cities you'll ever encounter, and there is no shortage of bars, clubs, dance halls, and open air venues featuring live performances of Brazil's myriad musical styles. Since Cariocas rarely listen to music without succumbing to the urge to move their bodies, most of these places feature dancing as well. For those who prefer a more globalized beat, the city has its share of nightclubs and discos, although in terms of contemporary sounds, São Paulo has the advantage. Although most of Centro shuts down after happy hour, the more traditional bohemian *bairros* of Santa Teresa and Lapa, and more recently the old port zone *bairros* of Saúde and Gamboa, have been reclaimed by new bohos

who flock to hear samba, *chorinho, forró,* and other homegrown melodies. The swankier watering holes and night spots of the Zona Sul offer more internationally urban brands of fun, albeit with a decidedly bossa nova twist.

Centro

Centro doesn't have much nightlife to speak of. However, amid its narrow old streets are some of the city's oldest and most atmospheric *botequins,* which fill up when happy hour rolls around. Accompanying the ongoing revitalization of the port zone, the adjacent neighborhoods of Saúde and Gamboa, which have long been a hotbed of Afro-Brazilian culture, are earning accolades as the next Lapa.

BARS
Adega do Timão (Rua Visconde de Itaboaraí 10, tel. 21/2516-91255, noon-midnight Tues.-Sun.) is a charming little bar decorated with nautical gear and a fancy crystal chandelier thrown in for good measure. Its proximity to the Centro Cultural Banco do Brasil and Espaço Cultura dos Correios has made it an obligatory beer stop for the culture crowd.

Bar Luiz (Rua da Carioca 39, tel. 21/2262-6900, www.barluiz.com.br, 11am-8pm Mon., 11am-10pm Tues.-Fri., 11am-6pm Sat.) is a classic Carioca *botequim* with a German accent—and menu, including a famous potato salad as well as various sausages and schnitzels.

Amarelinho (Praça Floriano 55-B, Cinelândia, tel. 21/2240-8434, www.amarelinhodacinelandia.com.br, 11am-2am daily) is Cinelândia's most famous yellow-tiled outdoor bar for people-watching and monument-gazing. Close by, **Villarino** (Av. Calógeras 6, Loja B, tel. 21/2240-9634, www.villarino.com.br, noon-10pm Mon.-Fri.) was a favorite haunt of a midcentury bohemian crowd that included Tom Jobim and Vinicius de Moraes, who used it as their private clubhouse. Today the retro *uisqueria* (whiskey bar) with its scarlet banquettes attracts a suit-and-tie crowd who alternate whiskey shots with bites of prosciutto and brie sandwiches.

Gay Rio

While Rio's vibe is quite gay friendly, few specifically gay venues exist. GLS (a Brazilian slang term for *gay, lesbica, e simpatisante*; i.e., gay friendly) spaces rule, with gays, lesbians, and heteros mixing socially. For more info about Rio's gay scene, visit www.riogaylife.com.

CENTRO
Cine Ideal (Rua da Carioca 62, tel. 21/2221-1984, http://cineideal.com.br, 11:30pm-close Fri.-Sat., cover R$25-30) is a disco with bars and a rooftop lounge.

PORT ZONE
The Week (Rua Sacadura Cabral 150, Saúde, tel. 21/2253-1020, www.week.com.br, midnight-close Sat., cover R$40-60) is a more massive and upscale São Paulo import.

LAPA
Buraco da Lacraia (Rua André Cavalcanti 58, tel. 21/2221-1984, http://buracodalacraia.com.br, 11pm-close Fri.-Sat., cover R$30-40) showcases drag shows, videoke contests, snooker, and electronic games. The beer is fantastically cheap.

IPANEMA
The high-profile strip of Ipanema beach stretching from Posto 8 to Posto 9 (nicknamed "Farme Gay") is home to beach *barracas* flying rainbow flags and the toned outlines of well-oiled "Barbies" (as muscle men are called). The street perpendicular to the beach, **Rua Farme de Amoedo** also attracts a gay crowd.

 Tô'Nem Aí (Rua Farme de Amoedo 87-A, tel. 21/2247-8403, www.tounemai.com.br, noon-3am daily) is a laid-back bar that draws a mixed crowd and offers great views of the action.

 Galeria Café (Rua Teixeira de Melo 31, tel. 21/2523-8250, www.galeriacafe.com.br, 10:30pm-close Wed.-Sat., noon-8pm Sun., cover R$28-38), one street over, is a hip, hybrid space sheltering a café and art gallery. At night, it holds sizzling *festas* that reel in a trendy crowd.

COPACABANA
The gay crowd has conquered a prize strip of beach, on the doorstep of the Copacabana Palace, baptized "Praia da Bolsa" (Handbag Beach).

 The **Rainbow** (noon-close daily) kiosk is a haven for Rio's transgendered community, who often perform in between caipis and pizza slices.

 Le Boy (Rua Raul Pompéia 102, tel. 21/2513-4993, www.leboy.com.br, 11pm-close Tues.-Sun., cover R$15-25) is Rio's classic and notorious temple of gaydom. This enormous club offers go-go boys, a *quarto escuro* (dark room), and Tuesday's Strip Nights.

 La Cueva (Rua Miguel Lemos 51, tel. 21/2267-1367, www.boatelacueva.com.br, 11pm-close, R$20) means "The Cave," which describes this dim, yet friendly basement lair where the entrance fee earns you two drinks.

LIVE MUSIC
Trapiche Gamboa (Rua Sacadura Cabral 155, Saúde, tel. 21/2516-0868, www.trapiche-gamboa.com, 6:30pm-close Tues.-Fri., 8pm-close Sat., cover R$12-20) was a pioneer when it opened in 2004. Occupying a handsomely restored 19th-century warehouse, it still offers some of the best live samba performances in town. Nearby, "Pedra do Sal" is the name of the gigantic chunk of granite anchoring the historic **Largo João da Baiana** (Rua Argemiro Bulcão, Gamboa, 7:30pm-close Mon., Wed., and Fri.), site of a former slave market as well as the believed birthplace of Carioca samba. It's a picturesque place to hear the vibrant *rodas de samba* pounded out by master sambistas.

Gafieiras were originally ballrooms where Rio's working classes danced the night away. They sprang up in Centro during the 1920s; by 1930, there were more than 450. Sadly, the sole survivor still hosting ballroom dancing is **Centro Cultural Estudantina Musical** (Praça Tiradentes 79, tel. 21/2232-1149, www.estudantinamusical.com.br, 7pm-1am Wed., 8pm-1am Fri., 10pm-2am Sat., cover R$15-20), whose decor conjures up its 1928 beginnings. Apart from orchestras playing traditional ballroom ditties (usually Sat.), you'll hear live bands playing samba, *choro,* and jazz. The mixed crowd includes people of all ages.

Lapa

Lapa is the city's undisputed hot spot to listen and dance to live music. Starting Thursday, its many bars, clubs, and narrow streets (particularly Rua Joaquim Silva) pulse with a variety of rhythms, revelers from every Carioca *bairro,* and tourists eager to samba. Although not quite as edgy as it used to be, Lapa still rules Rio's musical roost.

BARS

Like Centro, Lapa has some wonderful old *botequins.* **Bar Brasil** (Av. Mem de Sá 90, tel. 21/2509-5943, noon-midnight Mon.-Fri., 11:30am-6pm Sat.) is a neighborhood institution, serving German food such as *eisbein, kassler,* and sauerkraut—perfect between sips of frothy beer. The canvases on the walls are by Chilean artist Jorge Selarón, who is responsible for the mosaic-covered staircase that leads up to Santa Teresa. **Barzinho** (Rua do Lavradio 170, Lapa, tel. 21/2221-4709, www.barzinho, 6pm-2am Tues.-Wed., 6pm-3am Thurs., 6pm-4am Fri.-Sat.) opened in late 2013. This dimly lit hipster haunt provides an alternative to Lapa's trademark samba-inflected grittiness with bright neon colors and pulsing DJ-spun electronica. Events range from pop-up theater to performance art, while classic bar grub gets a sophisticated lease on life.

LIVE MUSIC AND NIGHTCLUBS

In Lapa's streets and renovated old buildings you'll encounter an astonishing diversity of music, and new bars and clubs are opening all the time. The majority are on Rua do Lavradio and Rua Mem de Sá. For listings and schedules, check out www.lanalapa.com.br.

One of the city's most enchanting bars, **Rio Scenarium** (Rua do Lavradio 20, tel. 21/3147-9000, www.rioscenarium.com.br, 6:30pm-2:30am Tues-Sat., cover R$20-35) is perpetually packed. If it has lost some of its cachet (lots of gringos trying to samba), it has retained its unique charm. Located on Lapa's antiques row, Rio Scenarium's three floors are full of antiques, which are rented out to film and TV productions—you can sit, sprawl, and lounge on certain pieces while others are merely eye candy. On most nights, top names in samba, *choro,* and *forró* perform. Arrive early (before 8pm) or reserve a table.

Carioca da Gema (Rua Mem de Sá 79, tel. 21/2221-0043, www.barcariocadagema. com.br, 6pm-close Mon.-Fri., 8pm-close Sat., cover R$25-30) is a classic spot to listen to top-quality samba and *choro* performed by big names and rising stars. The ambiance is warm and rustic, and there is a copious menu. **Clube dos Democráticos** (Rua do Riachuelo 91-93, Lapa, tel. 21/2252-4611, www.clubedosdemocraticos.com.br, 6pm-close Wed.-Sat., 8pm-close Sun., cover R$15-35) has been around since 1867. Members were a forward-thinking republican and abolitionist bunch whose bashes were legendary well into the 1940s. Today, dance soirees are held regularly in the vast ballroom. Music ranges from samba to *choro,* and the crowd is young.

In Carioca-ese, "40°" refers to the temperature (in Celsius) that descends on the city in the heat of summer. The name is apt: **Lapa 40°** (Rua Riachuelo 97, Lapa, tel. 21/3970-1329, www.lapa40graus.com.br, 6pm-4am daily, cover R$15-35) is one of Lapa's perennial hot spots. More than a bar or nightclub, it is a four-floor entertainment complex out-fitted with a bar, a ballroom, and a stage for live shows as well as a *tabacaria* (for smoking cigars), a *uisqueiria* (for doing whiskey shots), and dart boards. Oh, and if you get bored, there is an entire floor outfitted with 30 pool and billiard tables.

Santa Teresa
BARS
The unpretentious bars of "Santa" lure an al-ternative crowd charmed by the laid-back vibe of this boho *bairro*. Inspired by the typically rustic bars of Minas Gerais, **Bar do Mineiro** (Rua Paschoal Carlos Magno 99, tel. 21/2221-9227, 11am-1am Tues.-Sat., 11am-midnight Sun.) is a charmingly old-fashioned *botequim* accessorized with black-and-white photos and miniature wooden *bondes*.

Opened in 1919, **Armazém São Thiago** (Rua Áurea 26, tel. 21/2232-0822, www.arma-zemsaothiago.com.br, noon-midnight Mon.-Sat., noon-10pm Sun.), also known as Bar do Gomes, was once a general store that sold *secos e molhados* (dry goods and spirits). The *mol-hados* persevered, and today the dark wood shelves and cabinets are stacked sky-high with bottles and cases of wine and *cachaça*. A wooden fridge, marble-topped tables, art deco fixtures, and jocular waiters round out the retro pleasures. The clientele is made up of spirited locals.

Flamengo and Laranjeiras
Flamengo and Laranjeiras are home to some of the city's most traditional watering holes, where you can eat and drink well while soak-ing up authentic Carioca atmosphere.

BARS
A Flamengo favorite, **Belmonte** (Praia do Flamengo 300, tel. 21/2552-3349, 9am-4am daily) gets so busy in the late afternoons that customers stand and balance their cups on shiny metal barrels of beer. Although other locations have opened throughout the city, this original bar, opened in 1952, is the most atmospheric.

LIVE MUSIC
Casa Rosa (Rua Alice 550, Laranjeiras, tel. 21/2557-2562, www.casarosa.com.br, 11pm-close Fri.-Sat., 5pm-close Sun., cover R$10-30) is quite literally pink (a shocking one at that), but from the turn of the 20th century to the late 1980s its chromatic association was red: It was the town's most famous bordello, fre-quented by Laranjeiras's resident politicians, magnates, and military officers. Now one of Rio's coolest cultural centers, on weekends it rocks with live music and dance *festas* such as Friday's Baile Alice and Sunday's famous Feijoada do Projeto Raiz.

Botafogo, Cosme Velho, and Urca
BARS
Bar Urca (Rua Cândido Gaffré 205, Urca, tel. 21/2295-8744, www.barurca.com.br, 7am-11pm Mon.-Sat., 9am-9pm Sun.) is among the most scenic *botequins* in Rio, with a bewitch-ing view over the Baía de Guanabara. The up-stairs dining room functions as a restaurant whose menu emphasizes fish and seafood dishes, but you can also savor *petiscos* such as grilled sardines while soaking up the sun out on the seawall (many locals bring their own beach chairs). Amidst Botafogo's blossoming alternative bar scene, **Comuna** (Rua Sorocaba 585, Botafogo, tel. 21/3253-8797, http://co-muna.cc, 6pm-2am Tues.-Thurs., 6pm-4am Fri.-Sat., 6pm-midnight Sun.) is one of the coolest. The brainchild of four university pals, this hybrid cultural space is an unpre-tentious and friendly place to tap into Rio's creative pulse.

NIGHTCLUBS
A pioneer of Rio's alternative music and party scene, **Casa da Matriz** (Rua Henrique Novaes 107, Botofago, tel. 21/2266-1014, http://beta. matrizonline.com.br/casadamatriz, 9pm-midnight Tues., 8pm-5am Wed., 11pm-6am Thurs.-Sat., cover R$15-30) hosts some of the most happening dance parties in town, cour-tesy of a roster of house DJs. Wander around the historic house (decked out so it feels like a

bonafide house party), where you can play arcade games or flake out on a sofa. Arrive and leave early to avoid crazy long lines.

Copacabana and Leme

Copa throbs at night, but more as a result of red-light district action on Avenida Atlântica and the oceanfront restaurants and bars crammed with international tourists. Nonetheless, there are a few exceptional enclaves as well as the *quiosques* (kiosks) that strategically line the beach itself.

BARS

Cervantes (Av. Prado Junior 335, Copacabana, tel. 21/2275-6147, www.restaurantecervantes.com.br, noon-4am Sun. and Tues.-Thurs., noon-6am Fri.-Sat.) is one of Copa's favorite *botequins,* especially after a night of carousing. The house specialties are the impossibly thick sandwiches— most feature *abacaxi,* a native species of pineapple.

Bip Bip (Rua Almirante Gonçalves 50, Copacabana, Loja D, tel. 21/2267-9696, 7pm-1am daily) is a tiny hole-in-the-wall *botequim* with two saving graces: its location on a quiet Copa street, which allows tables and chairs to be arranged outside, and terrific musical jams by top Carioca samba, *choro,* and bossa nova performers. Utterly unpretentious, "Bip" is a welcome antidote to Copa's touristy oceanfront bars.

NIGHTCLUBS

Fosfobox (Rua Siqueira Campos 143, 22-A, Copacabana, tel. 21/2548-7498, www.fosfobox.com.br, 11pm-close Tues.-Sun., R$20-50) is one of the Zona Sul's only underground basement clubs. Depending on your spatial sensibilities, "Fosfo" is either intimate or claustrophobic, but the upstairs Fosfobar is definitely conducive to mellowing out. Spun by top national DJs, the soundtrack ranges from rock to funk to techno. The scene is Copa cool with a gritty, industrial edge.

Ipanema and Leblon

Both Ipanema and Leblon possess a vibrant nightlife that runs the gamut from laid-back, beloved sidewalk *botequins* to stylish bars, lounges, and a few nightclubs that attract an eternally fashionable crowd.

BARS

Jobi (Rua Ataulfo de Paiva 1166-B, Leblon, tel. 21/2274-0547, 10am-4am Sun.-Thurs., 10am-6am Fri.-Sat.) is a classic Leblon address, long frequented by artists, journalists, and intellectuals. It's perennially chosen as one of the city's top bars due to the quality of its *chope* and flavorful *petiscos.* Arrive early if you want a table.

Close by, **Bracarense** (Rua José Linhares 85, Leblon, tel. 21/2294-3549, 7am-midnight Mon.-Sat., 9am-10pm Sun.) is quite tiny, but the surrounding sidewalk at this laid-back neighborhood bar overflows with tables and stools. The *petiscos* here are justly celebrated.

If you're feeling beer-weary, head to the **Academia da Cachaça** (Rua Conde da Bernadote 26, Leblon, tel. 21/2529-2680, www.academiadacachaca.com.br, noon-2:30am daily) to savor one of the city's most famous caipirinhas. Lured by the hundreds of bottles of Brazil's national liquor on display (and available for purchase), you might also want to sample some of the finer *pingas* on the menu.

If you can't afford to splurge on a room at the Philippe Starck-designed Hotel Fasano, the next best thing is a cocktail in its supremely sophisticated lounge, **Barreto-Londra** (Av. Vieira Souto 80, Ipanema, tel. 21/3202-4000, www.hotelfasano.com.br, 8pm-1am Mon.-Wed., 8pm-4am Thurs.-Sat.), one of *the* places to see and be seen in the Zona Sul (reservations recommended). Trendiness aside, the warm brick walls, inviting leather sofas, elegant service, and a mean apple martini will have you mellow in no time.

LIVE MUSIC

Studio RJ (Av. Vieira Souto 110, Ipanema, tel. 21/2523-1204, www.studiorj.org, 9pm-close Tues.-Sat., 7pm-close Sun., cover R$25-50) offers a compelling mélange of homegrown and imported bands and DJs.

Tuesday night's Jazzmania has a loyal following. Rivaling the superb acoustics are dreamy views of Ipanema beach.

NIGHTCLUBS

Melt (Rua Rita Ludolf 47, Leblon, www.melt-bar.com.br, tel. 21/2249-9309, 10pm-4am Tues.-Sat., cover R$30-50) is utterly Leblon: sleek, chic, and globalized, just like the toned and tanned crowd that works up a glow on the dance floor. The musical selection—ranging from samba rock to hip-hop—is courtesy of a handful of rotating DJs. Creative dishes are served in the candlelit downstairs lounge.

Lagoa and Jardim Botânico
QUIOSQUES

With its stunning views of Corcovado and many *quiosques* (kiosks), Lagoa has become quite a scene. One of the most imaginative is Palaphita Kitch (Av. Epitácio Pessoa, Kiosk 20, Parque do Cantagalo, Lagoa, tel. 21/2227-0837, www.palaphitakitch.com.br, 6pm-1am Sun.-Thurs., 6pm-3am Fri.-Sat.), where Zona Sul cool meets the Amazon rain forest with lounge furniture made from reforested wood; at night, the place is lit by torches. For a taste of Bahia, head to OkeKa Baiana Tem (Kiosk 14, Epitácio Pessoa, Lagoa, tel. 21/8297-9766, www.okekabaianatem.com.br, 5pm-midnight Tues.-Fri., 2pm-midnight Sat., 8:30am-midnight Sun.). Amidst Catholic-Candomblé iconography, try tasty, if pricey, *acarajés* (crunchy black-eyed pea fritters) and *moquecas* (fish or seafood stews).

BARS

Overlooking the Lagoa, Bar Lagoa (Av. Epitácio Pessoa 1674, Lagoa, tel. 21/2523-1135, 6pm-2am Mon.-Fri., noon-2am Sat.-Sun.) is a beloved *botequim* whose art deco interior hasn't changed much since the 1930s. It was originally named Bar Berlin; the owner strategically changed its name during World War II, but the kitchen continues to serve hearty yet simple German fare.

Worthwhile for vittles and views is Lagoon (Av. Borges de Medeiros 1424, Lagoa,

www.lagoon.com.br, noon-2am, daily), a glistening entertainment complex that's home to cinemas and a musical supper club.

Gávea

The area known as Baixa Gávea has been a nocturnal hot spot for years, luring young Zona Sulistas to the lively bars fanning out from Praça Santos Dumont.

BARS

Braseiro da Gávea (Praça Santos Dumont 116, Gávea, tel. 21/2239-7494, noon-1am Sun.-Thurs., noon-3am Fri.-Sat.) is one of the most traditional *botequins* in the area. It serves up a delicious charcoal-grilled *picanha* (rump-steak) chicken with fries to satiate late-night hunger pangs.

NIGHTCLUBS

00 (Av. Padre Leonel França 240, Gávea, tel. 21/2540-8041, www.00site.com.br, 10pm-5am Tues.-Sat., 5pm-2am Sun., cover R$20-50), or "Zero Zero" (as it is pronounced) is located inside Rio's planetarium, and the likes of Mick Jagger and Javier Bardem have been cropping up amid the usual bevy of wealthy young Zona Sulistas and TV celebs—but it isn't star-gazing that makes this one of Rio's top nightspots. The stylish space is the real attraction: Merging outdoor gardens and an Asian fusion restaurant with an indoor lounge and dance floor, 00 oozes glammy sophistication. To keep clients on their well-pedicured toes, the tunes are eclectic and vary from house to '80s and '90s memorabilia, with guest DJs taking charge of frequent *festas*.

SHOPPING

The best things to buy in Rio (as opposed to elsewhere) are Brazilian beach fashions and surf wear, antiques, CDs, DVDs, and vinyl by classic and contemporary musicians, along with traditional percussion instruments. Precious and semiprecious stones are a classic purchase. You can also find traditional arts and crafts from all over the country.

Shopping Malls

Rio's *shoppings* are more than just malls: They are microcosms where Cariocas can shop till they drop, as well as wander, gossip, flirt, read, eat, check out a movie or play, and even go skating. Depending on the neighborhood, the clientele, shops, and ambiance vary widely. Hours of operation are always 10am-10pm Monday-Saturday, 3pm-9pm Sunday.

Shopping Rio Sul (Rua Lauro Müller 116, Botafogo, tel. 21/2122-8070, www.riosul. com.br) is one of the oldest and most popular *shoppings*. Its convenient location in Botafogo, close to the tunnel entrance to Copacabana, means that every single bus under the sun passes by.

The title for the chicest *shopping* in town goes to the **São Conrado Fashion Mall** (Estrada da Gávea 899, São Conrado, tel. 21/2111-4444, www.scfashionmall.com.br), a small but sleek mall with tropical foliage and skylights. The boutiques are all *feshun* (Carioca-speak for "fashion"), meaning tasteful and pricey.

Giving São Conrado a serious run for its *reais* is **Shopping Leblon** (Av. Afrânio Melo Franco 290, Leblon, tel. 21/2430-5122, www. shoppingleblon.com.br). Befitting its Leblon address, it is a beautiful place for beautiful people, with 200 stylish stores, cinemas, and a cultural center; a food court boasts stunning views of Lagoa Rodrigo de Freitas and Corcovado.

Located in a suburban neighborhood, **Barra Shopping** (Av. das Américas 4666, Barra da Tijuca, tel. 21/4003-4131, www.barrashopping.com.br) is the most massive of Rio's malls, with more than 500 stores.

Antiques

As the former imperial and republican capital of Brazil, Rio offers hidden treasures— if you have the patience to find them. **Shopping dos Antiquários** (Rua Siqueira Campos 143, Copacabana, tel. 21/2255-3461, 10am-7pm Mon.-Sat.) is a slightly beat-up, weirdly futuristic shopping center—Rio's first—dating from the 1960s. Its more than 70 antiques stores specialize in everything from colonial furniture, baroque sacred art, and antique dolls to art deco dishware and Bakelite jewelry.

Rio's other antiques mecca is Lapa's **Rua do Lavradio.** Alongside classic antiques stores and secondhand shops are boutiques specializing in early to mid-20th-century Brazilian designs and furnishings such as **Ateliê e Movelaria Belmonte** (Rua do Lavradio 34, Lapa, tel. 21/2507-6873, www. ateliebelmonte.com.br, 9am-6pm Mon.-Fri., 11am-2pm Sat.) and **Mercado Moderno** (Rua do Lavradio 130, Lapa, tel. 21/2508-6083, 9am-6pm Mon.-Fri., 9am-3pm Sat.). On the first Saturday afternoon of every month, the local merchants' association organizes the **Feira do Rio Antigo,** in which all the stores on Rua Lavradio join together with other antiques dealers for an open-air market.

Arts and Crafts

Neither Rio nor the surrounding state has much to boast of in terms of folk art or traditional crafts. However, if you won't be traveling to other parts of Brazil, there are a few recommended boutiques where you can pick up some authentic *artesanato.* The snug interior of **La Vereda** (Rua Almirante Alexandrino 428, Santa Teresa, tel. 21/2507-0317, www.lavereda.com.br, 10am-8pm daily) showcases a well-chosen collection of traditional art and handicrafts from all over Brazil as well as contemporary works by Santa's many neighborhood artists. **Brasil & Cia** (Rua Maria Quitéria 27, Ipanema, tel. 21/2267-4603, www.brasilecia.com.br, 10am-7pm Mon.-Fri., 10am-4pm Sat.) works with a hand-picked group of talented artists from all over the country who create decorative objects that, while steeped in regional traditions, also bear the individual mark of their creators. The owner of **Pé de Boi** (Rua Ipiranga 55, Laranjeiras, tel. 21/2285-4395, www.pedeboi. com.br, 9am-7pm Mon.-Fri., 9am-1pm Sat.) has an encyclopedic knowledge of Brazilian folk art; most of the vivid sculptures, toys, and decorative objects on display in this gallery space have been culled from the Northeast, Amazon, and Minas Gerais.

Books and Music

Livrarias aren't just for reading or browsing, but for seeing and being seen. They fill up on weekends and at night with real and pretend intellectuals who spill into the delightful cafés and bistros that coexist with stacks of books and magazines. Events include author readings and live performances of jazz, samba, *chorinho,* and bossa nova—enhancing the romance factor. The best *livrarias* are in Ipanema and Leblon.

The main branch of **Livraria da Travessa** (Rua Visconde de Pirajá 572, Ipanema, tel. 21/3205-9002, www.travessa.com.br, 9am-midnight Mon.-Sat., 11am-midnight Sun.) has an extensive collection of books about Rio (some in English) as well as lots of CDs and DVDs. Its sleek mezzanine bistro, **Bazaar,** has delicious things to nibble on. You'll find other branches in Centro and Barra. Cozy **Livraria Argumento** (Rua Dias Ferreira 417, Leblon, tel. 21/2239-5294, www.livraria-argumento.com.br, 9am-midnight Mon.-Sat., 11am-midnight Sun.) is like a second home to many Leblon residents.

Many *livrarias* have good, if rapidly shrinking, CD and DVD sections devoted to Brazilian music. Inside the Paço Imperial, **Arlequim** (Praça XV de Novembro 48, Centro, tel. 21/2533-4359, www.arlequim.com.br) is a welcoming store with a rich selection of Brazilian music available in CD, DVD, and Blu-ray. They also stage live musical performances.

Biscoito Fino (www.biscoitofino.com.br) is an indie record label whose mission is to produce intelligent and innovative MPB (*biscoito fino,* or fine cookie, is a Brazilian expression meaning high quality). Biscoito Fino embraces promising vanguard artists as well as consecrated legends who are weary of corporate labels, and is also involved in uncovering lost relics from Brazil's musical past (including some amazing *choro* recordings). It also launched Biscoitinho, specializing in popular Brazilian music for children. You can also find Biscoito Fino kiosks in Shopping Rio Sul and Shopping da Gávea.

Maracatu Brasil (Rua Ipiranga 49, Laranjeiras, tel. 21/2557-4754, www.maracatubrasil.com.br, noon-8pm Mon.-Fri.) combines a music school and recording studio with a great array of new and used traditional, handcrafted, and modern Brazilian percussion instruments that can be rented as well as purchased. When you drop in, check to see who's performing in the small courtyard out back; talented percussionists often give happy-hour shows. And if you're interested in learning to play drums in a samba *bloco,* sign up for lessons taught by top-notch musicians.

Cachaça and Cigars

A beloved relic of Copa's heyday, **Charutaria Lollô** (Av. Nossa Senhora de Copacabana 683, Copacabana tel. 21/2235-0625, 7am-11pm daily) has been the place to go for a smoke and a *cafezinho* since it first opened in 1952. Savor both on the spot, or do like Tom Jobim, who strolled by every Sunday to buy a box of his favorite cigars, and make your purchases to go. **Garapa Doida** (Rua Carlos Goís 234, Loja F, Leblon, tel. 21/2274-8186, 11am-8pm Mon.-Fri., 11am-5pm Sat.) reunites more than 150 brands of *pinga* from all over Brazil; all have been certified by government institutions and approved by connoisseurs (clients are also encouraged to sample the wares). Among the rarest is Senador, from Minas Gerais, which is aged for 18 years in barrels made of native *garapa* wood.

Clothing and Accessories

Ipanema's tree-lined streets are stuffed with boutiques selling the latest creations from Brazilian and Carioca designers. The largest concentration of stores can be found on Rua Barão da Torre, Rua Gárcia d'Avila, Rua Anibal de Mendonça, and Rua Visconde de Pirajá, where many *galerias* (similar to micro-malls) offer hidden treasures.

Rio fashion is all about beachwear. Men can indulge in surf wear and some summery casual wear (jeans and T-shirts), but otherwise Carioca designers cater more to women, with clingy, sexy lines and designs in bright colors with interesting details. **Blue Man** (www.blueman.com.br), **Lenny** (www.lenny.com.br), **Bum Bum** (www.bumbum.com.br), **Salinas** (www.salinascompras.com.br), and **Rosa Chá** (www.rosacha.com.br) are all Carioca labels whose eternally fashionable *sungas* and bikinis are sold at their various brand-name boutiques around town as well as at *shoppings* such as Rio Sul, Leblon, and São Conrado Fashion Mall.

Women will also find lots of great shoes — the higher-heeled, the better—while both sexes will delight in the variety of funky flip-flops available. For an amazing selection of Havaianas, head to **Havaianas** (Rua Farme de Amoedo 76, Ipanema, tel. 21/2267-7395, http://br.havaianas.com, 9am-7pm Mon.-Fri., 10am-7pm Sat., 10am-6pm Sun.), where you can slip into flip-flops ranging from basic to customized. Aside from this Ipanema outpost, you'll find more than 40 stores throughout the city.

If you're young and male, you'll make out better at **Galeria River** (Rua Francisco Otaviano 67, Arpoador, tel. 21/2247-8387, www.galeriariver.com.br, 9am-8pm Mon.-Sat.), an alternative enclave whose tiny but well-stocked stores are devoted entirely to the art, lifestyle, and fashion of surf. This is a great place to get a surfer haircut, a tattoo or three, or to energize yourself with a super-healthy *vitamina,* full of fruit juices and medicinal herbs.

For an urban style with latent beach possibilities, check out streetwear brands with a distinctly Carioca flavor, such as **Totem** (Rua Visconde de Pirajá 500, Ipanema, tel. 21/2540-9977 www.totempraia.com.br) and **Osklen** (Rua Maria Quiteria 86, Ipanema, tel. 21/2227-2911, www.osklen.com).

Gilson Martins (Rua Visconde de Pirajá 462, Ipanema, tel. 21/2227-6178, www.gilsonmartins.com.br) designs ingenious Carioca bags in comic-book colors that are as sculptural as they are functional.

Jewelry

Rio's equivalent of Tiffany's is **H. Stern** (Rua Visconde de Pirajá 490, Ipanema, tel. 21/2274-3447, www.hstern.com.br, 10am-7pm Mon.-Fri., 10am-2pm Sat.). Its PR team sends flyers to basically every hotel in Rio offering to pick you up, take you to the Ipanema headquarters for a tour of their ateliers, and bring you back home again (hopefully with a small bag full of pricey rocks). Specialists in Brazil's precious and semiprecious stones, the jewelers here create innovative contemporary designs as well as more classic, conservative bling.

Antonio Bernardo (Rua Gárcia d'Avila 121, Ipanema, tel. 21/2512-7204, www.antoniobernardo.com.br, 10am-8pm Mon.-Fri., 10am-4pm Sat.) is a goldsmith, artist, and orchid lover (he adopted the Jardim Botânico's *orquidário*) who designs beautifully wrought contemporary jewelry. For something a little more eco-chic, consider a bio-bijou fashioned by Amazonas-born **Maria Oiticica** (http://loja.mariaoiticica.com.br). You'll find a boutique in Shopping Leblon.

Markets

Rio has some lively outdoor markets, most held on weekends. The most famous is Ipanema's **Feira Hippie** (Praça General Osório, Ipanema, 9am-6pm Sun.). It features a crowded but lively jumble-sale atmosphere that attracts an awful lot of tourists (and pickpockets) and is somewhat overrated. If you are in Centro between 9am and 5pm on a Saturday, you might enjoy browsing through the cornucopia of antiques and bric-a-brac on display at Praça XV's **Feira de Antiguidades.** On Sunday, the same goods migrate to Gávea's Praça Santos Dumont.

For more contemporary wares, head to **Babilônia Feira Hype,** which takes place on alternate weekends at the Lagoa's Clube Monte Líbano (Av. Borge de Medeiros 701, Leblon, www.babiloniafeirahype.com.br, 2pm-10pm every second Sat.-Sun., R$10). This fashion-forward market has an assortment of clothing, jewelry, and design pieces by up-and-coming Rio designers as well as outdoor eateries.

SPORTS AND RECREATION

Blessed with so many natural attractions, it is unsurprising that Cariocas are a pretty sporty bunch. Beach activities—everything from walking, jogging, and yoga to surfing, soccer, and volleyball—are very popular, as are radical sports, especially those that take advantage of the city's mountain peaks. The exuberantly green Floresta da Tijuca offers an oasis for athletes who want to commune with nature.

★ Floresta da Tijuca

Although the dense tropical forest that covers Rio's mountains possesses a primeval quality, the truth is that by the 19th century, the original Atlantic forest that had existed for thousands of years had been almost completely cleared to make way for sugar and coffee plantations. The deforestation was so dire that by the mid-1800s, Rio was facing an ecological disaster that menaced the city's water supply. Fortunately, inspired Emperor Dom Pedro II had a green conscience. In 1861, he ordered that 3,300 hectares be replanted with native foliage—the first example of government-mandated reforestation in Brazil's history. Over time, the forest returned to its original state, and today this urban rain forest boasts an astounding variety of exotic trees and animals ranging from jewel-colored hummingbirds to monkeys, squirrels, and armadillos.

Within the Floresta lies the largest urban park in Brazil, the Parque Nacional da Tijuca (tel. 21/2492-2252, www.parquedatijuca.com.br, 8am-5pm daily). Divided into four sectors, the most-visited is Serra da Carioca, which also has the best infrastructure. Better for walking and climbing are Pedras da Gávea e Bonita and Floresta da Tijuca. Floresta da Tijuca is home to the main visitor center, Praça Afonso Viseu (Estrada da Cascatinha 850, Tijuca), where you can buy maps and get guide recommendations. To get here, take the Metrô to Saens Pena, then hop on a bus to Barra da Tijuca, stopping at the main Alto da Boa Vista entrance. Near the entrance are three restaurants and a café. A second visitor center is at Parque Lage (Rua Jardim Botânico 414, Jardim Botânico), in Serra da Carioca.

The park has more than 100 walking trails—many quite easy—along with waterfalls, grottoes, and lookout points that offer stunning views of the city. The most spectacular are the Mesa do Imperador (Emperor's Table)—where Dom Pedro II liked to picnic with members of his court—and the Vista Chinesa. Although trails are well marked, explore the park in the company of a local or an organized group to avoid getting lost (or robbed). Customized tours in English are available; recommended outfits include Rio Hiking (tel. 21/2552-9204, www.riohiking.com.br) or Jungle Me (tel. 21/4105-7533, www.jungleme.com.br, R$150-200 pp).

Not far from the Tijuca entrance (accessible by foot, bus, or car), the Museu do Açude (Estrada do Açude 764, Alto da Boa Vista, tel. 21/3433-4990, www.museuscastromaya.com.br, 11am-5pm Wed.-Mon., R$2, free Thurs.) exhibits the art collection of wealthy industrialist Raymundo Ottoni de Castro Maya. The main treat, however, is the permanent installation space, which includes giant works by some of Brazil's most important contemporary artists.

Boating

Get out on the blue waters of the Baía da Guanabara. Saveiro's Tour (Av. Infante Dom Henrique, Marina da Glória, Glória, tel. 21/2225-6064, www.saveiros.com.br) rents out all types of seaworthy vessels as well as water skis. Those interested in a mini-cruise can charter a posh yacht that will take you up and down the coast to destinations such as Búzios, Ilha Grande, Angra dos Reis, and Paraty. A two-hour tour around the Baía da Guanabara costs R$50 pp.

Cycling

Rio has more than 300 kilometers (186 mi) of bike paths. Those in search of a languorous outing can take to the paths that line the br) specializes in nature hiking. Top tours include hikes in Floresta da Tijuca and along the unique and little-explored Zona Oueste beaches. Full-day tours cost around R$140-180 pp.

Companhia da Escalada (tel. 21/2567-7105, www.companhiadaescalada.com.br, R$100-160 pp) and **Climb in Rio** (tel. 21/2245-1108, www.climbinrio.com) organize rock-climbing classes and excursions for beginners and experts as well as multiday adventures to peaks throughout Rio state, such as the Serra dos Orgãos and Itatiaia. Half-day climbs average around R$220 pp.

Hang Gliding

The popularity of hang gliding in Rio is second only to surfing. A classic (and breathtaking) trip is to jump off Pedra Bonita (in the Parque Nacional da Tijuca) and glide down to the Praia do Pepino in São Conrado. Both **Just Fly** (tel. 21/2268-0565, http://justflyinrio.blogspot.com) and **Super Fly** (tel. 21/3322-2286, www.riosuperfly.com.br) charge around R$250 for the 15-minute thrill, including transportation to and from your hotel. Flights may be cancelled if weather conditions are less than ideal; schedule an early take-off for more leeway.

Surfing

To facilitate getting around town, the city ingeniously operates a special **Surf Bus** (tel. 21/8515-2289 or 21/9799-5039, www.surf-bus.com.br) equipped to deal with boards and dripping bodies. Leaving from Largo do Machado in Botafogo, it travels all the way down the coast from Copacabana to Prainha, departing at 7am, 10am, 1pm, and 4pm. Despite the fact that it's equipped with air-conditioning, a minibar, and a 29-inch TV that screens surfing DVDs, the cost is only R$5.

If you want to hone your technique, **Escola de Surf Rico de Souza** (Av. Lúcio Costa 3300, Barra, tel. 21/8777-7775, http://ricosurf.globo.com) offers daily surfing lessons at its headquarters (in front of Posto 4)

Copacabana beach

beaches (stretching from Flamengo to Leblon and then along Barra) and ring the Lagoa Rodrigo de Freitas. Hard-core jocks can take on the steep trails leading into the Floresta da Tijuca. You can rent bikes in many places along the Zona Sul beaches and around the Lagoa. A particularly wide range of models are available at **Bike & Lazer** (Rua Visconde de Pirajá 135-B, Ipanema, tel. 21/2267-7778, www.bikelazer.com.br, R$15 per hour), which has a second location in Laranjeiras near Largo do Machado (Rua das Laranjeiras 58, tel. 21/2285-7941). Kiosks surrounding Lagoa de Freitas also rent bikes (R$10 per hour).

Hiking and Climbing

Friendly, English-speaking mother-and-son team Denise Werneck and Gabriel operate **Rio Hiking** (tel. 21/2552-9204, www.riohiking.com.br). Expeditions in and around the city and surrounding state range from walks in the park to Iron Man-level challenges as well as biking, diving, and kayaking. **Jungle Me** (tel. 21/4105-7533, www.jungleme.com.

and at Prainha (Praia da Macumba) as well as equipment rental. Private lessons for both cost R$100 per hour; group lessons are considerably cheaper. To buy or rent surf equipment, check out the stores at **Galeria River** (Rua Francisco Otaviano 67, www.galeriariver.com.br).

Soccer

Brazil's favorite sport is also Rio's, and you'll see everyone from women to *favela* kids to beer-bellied seniors shooting and scoring, particularly on the beaches. To see the real deal, head to the largest *futebol* stadium in the world: **Maracanã** (Rua Professor Eurico Rabelo, Maracanã, tel. 0800-062-7222, www.maracana.com, R$30-60). Built in 1950 to host the World Cup and majorly revamped for the 2014 Cup, the stadium seats close to 80,000 people. Even if soccer leaves you cold, it's worth taking in a game for the sheer theatrics of the crowd, who toot whistles, beat drums, unfurl gigantic banners, and wield smoke bombs in team colors. When things aren't going well, fans shed tears, implore saints, and hurl death threats. When victory rears its head, it's more like a collective mini-Carnaval.

Rio's four biggest and most traditional teams are Flamengo, Fluminense, Botafogo, and Vasco da Gama. Each has its die-hard followers, but the most toxic rivalry of all is the legendary Flamengo-Fluminense ("Fla-Flu") match-up. Games are played throughout the week (usually Wed.-Thurs. nights and weekend afternoons). Avoid rabid fans on the bus by taking the Metrô or a taxi. **Be a Local** (tel. 21/9643-0366, http://bealocal.com) can score tickets and provide both local chaperones and gringo cohorts. During the day, Maracanã is open for 50-minute guided tours (9am-5pm daily, 8am-11am game days, R$10).

ACCOMMODATIONS

Hotels in Rio feel entitled to charge a lot for the (undisputed) pleasure of staying in the *Cidade Maravilhosa*, and you'll find scads of hotels catering to international visitors near the beaches of Copacabana, Ipanema, and Leblon. Copacabana has the most options, but many that line the beachfront of Avenida Atlântica are overpriced chains that (aside from high-end luxury hotels) offer fairly standard guest rooms in various states of decay. An increasing number have received well-overdue renovations, and a few classic hotels from Copa's 1950s heyday have been treated to makeovers.

Ipanema's accommodations veer between luxury beachfront and mediocre two-stars charging four-star prices. This has begun to shift thanks to some conscientious upgrading as well as the opening of several appealing B&Bs. The opening of atmospheric and affordable guesthouses, as well as boutique hotels in historic houses, is a welcome trend in other traditional residential *bairros* such as Botafogo, Gávea, Santa Teresa (especially), and even Leblon.

To meet the demands of the 2014 World Cup and 2016 Summer Olympics, Rio's hotel sector should have undertaken a major expansion spree. Apart from uninspiring chain hotels in Barra, it didn't. As a result, extremely high occupation rates are driving up prices. Rio's high season now lasts all year—except for New Year's and Carnaval, when rates skyrocket and advance reservations are essential.

Centro and Lapa

Centro and Lapa appeal more to business travelers than to sun worshippers who might find it frustrating to be so far from the glittering sands of Copacabana and Ipanema. Both are well served by Metrô and bus, so you can get anywhere you want fast, and prices are less expensive than in Zona Sul. On the downside, neither neighborhood is very safe (particularly Centro, which is deserted at night and on weekends), so be prepared to spend a lot on cab fare.

R$50-200

Hotel Belas Artes (Av. Visconde do Rio Branco 52, Centro, tel. 21/2252-6336, www.hotelbelasartes.com.br, R$140-180 d), in a handsome historic building in the heart of Centro, is a well-regarded hotel that offers simply furnished but spotless guest rooms with high ceilings and wooden floors—all for an unbeatable price. Expect some street noise.

R$200-400

The formerly down-and-out **Arcos Rio Palace** (Av. Mem de Sá 117, Lapa, tel. 21/2242-8116, www.arcosriopalacehotel.com. br, R$290 d) is now a safe, spotless, and comfortable hotel. Amenities include a swimming pool, sauna, fitness room, and friendly service. The real bonus is direct access to Lapa's vibrant nightlife (and noise); request a room on a top floor.

Santa Teresa

Bucolic and bohemian "Santa" provides a wonderful antidote to the Zona Sul beach scene, where visionary entrepreneurs are taking advantage of the abundance of atmospheric belle epoque villas and going the restoration route.

R$50-200

Possibly Rio's best hostel, **Santê Hostel** (Rua Felício dos Santos 62, tel. 21/8883-0164, www. hostelworld.com, R$180 d, R$32-37pp) offers a few communal and double rooms in a private family home full of creature comforts and whimsical details. Charming family members and staff take guests under their collective wing, and gigantic old windows, hardwood floors, a gorgeous tiled communal kitchen, and even a purring cat add value to an already great bargain.

Staying at eco-conscious, French-owned **Casa da Gente** (Rua Gonçalves Fontes 33, tel. 21/2232-2634, www.casadagente.com, R$175-265 d) is like crashing at the *casa* of your coolest aunt. You're handed a key and then have full run of the crazily vertical, four-story house with its art-infested nooks and crannies, communal kitchen, and surreal lawn-covered terrace overlooking Lapa (from which you're only steps away; be prepared for drifting ambient noise).

R$200-400

Casalegre Art Vila (Rua Monte Alegre 316, tel. 21/98670-6158, www.casalegre.com.br, R$200-290 d) channels Santa's artistic-boho vibe. Eight eccentric rooms in this delightfully rambling colonial mansion are full of art, antiques, and ambiance; some rooms have kitchenettes, where guests stay for weeks or even months at reduced rates. The casa doubles as a gallery space, and a courtyard café encourages mingling.

As laid-back, good-humored, and flawlessly efficient as its American expat owners, ★ **Casa Cool Beans B&B** (Rua Laurindo Santos Lobo 136, tel. 21/2262-0552, www.casacoolbeans.com, R$260-340 d) has 10 spacious rooms and chalets located near neighborhood hotspot Bar do Gomes. Perks range from giant plush towels to maple syrup with your breakfast pancakes, along with lush gardens and a pool. **Castelinho 38** (Rua Triunfo 38, tel. 21/2252-2549, www.castelinho38.com, R$250-340 d) occupies a delightfully Hollywoodesque castle built in the 1860s, complete with turrets and towers. Each of the 10 lovely guest rooms is named after a fruit tree or tropical plant. Wood floors, lofty ceilings, and lots of light reign, as does a hippie vibe: A "Well-Being" space allows guests to indulge in yoga, Pilates, and "sacred dances."

Experience life with the locals by staying as a guest in a private home. ★ **Cama e Café** (Rua Paschoal Carlos Magno 90, tel. 21/2225-4366, www.camaecafe.com.br, R$150-300) is a bed-and-breakfast network that links travelers and (often very interesting) residents. In Santa Teresa, you can choose from dozens of offerings based on factors such as cost, comfort, and common interests. Many of the hosts are artists and liberal professionals with at least a smattering of English and an impressive knowledge of the city.

R$400-600

The French owner of **Mama Ruisa** (Rua Santa Cristina 132, tel. 21/2242-1281, www. mamaruisa.com, R$500-650 d) ceaselessly combed antiques stores with the goal of creating an elegant and retro ambiance for this gleaming mansion's seven guest rooms, then added landscaped gardens punctuated by an inviting blue pool. The fabulous city views glimpsed through the trees are the only indication you're in Rio. Spa services (manicures, pedicures, massages) and chauffeured city tours are available.

OVER R$600

A former 200-year-old coffee plantation mansion, luxurious **Hotel Santa Teresa** (Rua Almirante Alexandrino 660, tel. 21/3382-0200, www.santa-teresa-hotel.com, R$850-1,700 d) was transformed into a swanky hotel in the 1920s. Today, the French-owned and -operated hotel is Rio's only member of the Relais & Châteaux hotel group. Seductive trappings include an infinity pool, lush gardens, a spa, and the romantic Bar dos Descasados. The restaurant, **Térèze,** racks up accolades for its inventive "New World" cuisine.

Glória and Catete

Lively and convenient Glória and Catete are somewhat frayed around the edges, but offer some very good deals if you're not too picky.

R$50-200

One of Glória's few accommodations options, the **Baron Garden** (Rua Barão de Guaratiba 195, Glória, tel. 21/2245-2749, www.barongarden.com, R$150-180 d, R$70 pp) is set at the top of a steep hill and offers 16 beds, including private doubles and an eight-bed dorm. While the trappings are hardly luxe, the house has plenty of character, and the arduous climb is compensated by the stunning views. Friendly owners cultivate a homey vibe conducive to rustling up meals in the gleaming kitchen or chilling out by the pool.

You've never seen an English B&B like the one built by former British war correspondent Bob Nadkarni. ★ **The Maze Inn** (Rua Tavares Bastos 414, Casa 66, Catete, tel. 21/2558-5547, http://jazzrio.com, R$150-180 d) features a labyrinth-like ensemble of curving concrete buildings adorned with Gaudí-esque mosaics and Nadkarni's artwork, all set amidst mountains as well as the surrounding *favela* of Tavares Bastos (though in terms of safety, the only shooting you'll encounter is TV and movie crews). The small suites are light on furnishings but heavy on atmosphere; there are also housekeeping units with living rooms and kitchens. You'll have difficulty tearing yourself away from the rooftop terrace, where Pão de Açúcar seems close enough to touch. Even if you don't check in, it's worth checking out the monthly Friday night jazz performances, which have become a cult event. Transportation up the hill is provided by frequent VW vans (R$3) and moto-taxis (R$4).

Botafogo, Cosme Velho, and Urca

R$50-200

Oztel (Rua Pinheiro Guimarães 91, Botafogo, tel. 21/3042-1853, www.oztel.com.br, R$120-150 d, R$49-57 pp) has a laid-back vibe that dovetails perfectly with its location on a tranquil residential street whose cool factor has intensified with the opening of the owners' nearby bar, **Meza.** Collective hostel rooms are airy and spotless, but the style quotient kicks in with the whimsically decorated, very affordable private rooms and extends to a lounge and hang-out area, where pop-up events are held. A young staff of hipsters (without the attitude) generously dole out insider travel tips.

R$200-400

Halfway up a winding (but easily walkable) road to Corcovado and camouflaged by a patch of Tijuca Forest, **O Veleiro** (Rua Mundo Novo 1440, Botafogo, tel. 21/2554-8980, www.oveleiro.com.br, R$240-280 d) is one of Rio's first and most restive B&Bs. Smoothly administered by a Canadian-Carioca couple as amiable as they are efficient, the historic house has three guest rooms, appealing living areas, a pool, and lush gardens that merge with the surrounding jungle. Monkeys, toucans, and hummingbirds bestow a delicious sense of being away from it all.

Copacabana and Leme
R$50-200

If you're young in age or spirit, but low on bucks, ★ **Lisetonga Hostel** (Laderia Ary Barroso, Casa 15, Leme, tel. 21/2541-0393, www.lisetongahostel.com, R$90 d, R$40-60 pp) is ideal. Occupying a castlelike villa a short but steep climb from Leme's beach, Lisetonga provides bunks and a warm communal ambience. Travelers can discover the city together with the help of the personable staff, then regroup around the bar in time for happy hour. Winding staircases, hammock-strewn courtyards, and a colorful kitchen have induced many to temporarily move in; reservations are advised.

R$200-400

It's five blocks from the beach, but those in search of a little piece of mind and a great deal will find **Hotel Santa Clara** (Rua Décio Villares 316, Copacabana, tel. 21/2256-2650, www.hotelsantaclara.com.br, R$210-240 d) in a location nicely removed from Copa's bustle (but adjacent to the Metrô). Try for guest rooms facing the front, particularly on the top floor, which are the brightest and breeziest.

On the same street, **SESC Copacabana** (Rua Domingos Ferreira 160, Copacabana, tel. 21/2548-1088, www.sescrio.org.br, R$360-430 d) is not only a great deal for Copa, but you get to stay in an architectural landmark designed by Oscar Niemeyer. Guest rooms are coolly minimalist, and those above the 10th floor offer terrific views of Corcovado.

R$400-600

Inaugurated in 1949, when Copa's glamour was peaking, the classy art deco facade of the **Olinda Rio Hotel** (Av. Atlântica 2230, Copacabana, tel. 21/2159-9000, www.olindariohotel.com, R$370-480 d) is a welcome contrast amidst a sea of high-rises. Step inside and the flashback continues: awash in Italian marble, Persian carpets, and crystal chandeliers,

the lobby oozes grandeur. Splurge for the oceanfront rooms with balconies.

Rio's only beachfront B&B (and a penthouse no less!), ★ **Rio Guesthouse** (Rua Francisco Sá 5, Copacabana, tel. 21/2521-8586, www.rioguesthouse.com.br, R$360-530 d) consists of a handful of comfortable, color-coded rooms and Art Deco salons with glass walls and terraces that gape upon Copacabana's hypnotic crescent. Hostess Marta is like the Carioca mom you wish you always had.

OVER R$600

One of the most legendary hotels in the world and a national landmark, the refurbished ★ **Copacabana Palace** (Av. Atlântica 1702, Copacabana, tel. 21/2548-7070, www.copacabanapalace.com, R$1,490-2,100 d) is as famous as the beach it sits on. When this dazzling white hotel was constructed in 1923, Copacabana was little more than an unspoiled strip of sand surrounded by mountains. A decade later, the Palace played a prominent role in the RKO classic *Flying Down to Rio,* the first film to pair Fred Astaire and Ginger Rogers. Since then, the Palace has continued to attract a cavalcade of international stars, jet-setters, heads of state, and royalty without losing a shred of its elegance. When not holed up in the luxury of their poshly furnished rooms, these privileged guests can often be spotted lounging around the Olympic-size pool, getting pampered in the spa, playing a few sets on the rooftop tennis court, or dining in one of the two highly reputed restaurants, Cipriani and Pérgula. The extravagant cost is worth every penny.

The Palace's most serious rival is the **Sofitel Rio de Janeiro** (Av. Atlântica 4240, Copacabana, tel. 21/2525-1232, www.sofitel.com, R$750-1,250 d). What this ultramodern, somewhat overpriced hotel lacks in charm and pedigree, it tries to make up for with a dazzling array of enticing extras. The swanky guest rooms are outfitted with plasma TVs, immense beds, and balconies overlooking the entire length of Copacabana beach. Two strategically positioned rooftop pools allow you to catch both morning and afternoon rays. Other bonuses include Le Pré Catalan, considered one of Rio's top French restaurants, and a location on the frontier between Copa and Ipanema.

One of Avenue Atlântica's best values, the Arena Copacabana (Av. Atlântica 2064, Copacabana, tel. 21/3034-1501, http://arena-hotel.com.br, R$560-880 d) is a polished affair; contemporary rooms are tricked out with the latest modern conveniences (though Wi-Fi is *not* free). The more expensive ones have sea views, but all can indulge in the rooftop pool along with a sauna and fitness room.

Ipanema and Leblon

R$50-200

One Ipanema's best hostels, The Mango Tree (Rua Prudente de Moraes 594, Ipanema, tel. 21/2287-9255, www.mangotreehostel.com, R$170-240 d, R$60 pp) offers clean but basic accommodations in a restored 1930s villa only a block from Posto 9, Ipanema's hippest patch of sand. Small size combined with a "no noise after 10pm" rule dissuades late-night party animals, but plenty of socializing goes on in the common spaces, which include a deck hung with hammocks, a barbecue pit, and a garden with the mascot *mangueira* (mango tree).

Z.Bra Hostel (Av. Gal. San Martin 1212, Leblon, tel. 21/3596-2386, www.zbrahostel.com, R$140-175 d, R$55-60 pp) is a block from the beach (parasols are available), in the heart of the action. Rooms are small but stylishly efficient, and a loungey hang-out space sports delightfully mashed-up furnishings and a pre-party atmosphere nourished by the hostel bar. The gregarious staff can organize outings far beyond Leblon's borders.

R$200-400

One of Ipanema's only *pousadas,* Margarida's Pousada (Rua Barão da Torre 600, Ipanema tel. 21/2238-1840, www.margaridaspousada.com, R$270) is a three-story building whose basic yet homey rooms (for 2-4 people) are well cared for by kind,

no-nonsense owner Margarida. A big bonus is the coveted location midway between Ipanema beach and the Lagoa.

R$400-600

One of Ipanema's best value hotels, Ipanema Inn (Rua Maria Quitéria 27, Ipanema, tel. 21/2523-6093, http://ipanemainn.com.br, R$390-510 d) has a terrific location only half a block from the beach, yet that half-block makes a world of difference in terms of price. Quarters are tight, but the spotless guest rooms are modern and service is good. If you plan to spend most of your time on the beach, this is a convenient choice.

The Arpoador Inn (Rua Francisco Otaviano 177, Ipanema, tel. 21/2523-0060, http://arpoadorinn.com.br, R$390-610 d) is not only the most affordable beachfront hotel in Ipanema but is within spitting distance of Copacabana, and looks right onto the surfer's mecca of Praia do Arpoador. Rooms themselves are functional but not overly attractive—if you want a sea view, you'll have to pay a lot extra for it.

Brought to you by the same American duo who created Santa Teresa's Casa Cool Beans B&B, ★ Casa Cool Beans Flats (Rua Vinícius de Moraes 72, Ipanema, tel. 21/8204-1458, http://flats.casacoolbeans.com, R$350-670) is a revolutionary concept for Rio that straddles an *apart-hotel* with a B&B. Occupying the four floors of an atmospheric 1940s building, studio and one-bedroom suites are sunny, glossy, and modern. Amenities include daily housekeeping, breakfast vouchers for a local café, and the advice of co-owner David.

OVER R$600

The brainchild of two French expats, ★ Casa Mosquito (Rua San Roman 222, Ipanema, tel. 21/3586-5042, http://casamosquito.com, R$670-1,200 d) is an exquisite boutique-style guesthouse. Hidden on a steep street that climbs from Metrô Ipanema up to Morro do Pavão, views include both the *favela* and the beach. Inspired by iconic Brazilian personalities, decorated with Gallic panache, and dotted with patios, the rooms are split between a 1940s building and newer annex. Gourmet meals feature daily produce (breakfast not included).

A favorite of business execs, the **Promenade Palladium** (Av. General Artigas 200, Leblon, tel. 21/3171-7400, www. hotel-promenade-palladium.com, R$620-840 d) is comfortable if bland, with a prime Leblon location.

The Fasano family—which owns some of São Paulo's most celebrated high-class hotels and restaurants—procured Philippe Starck to oversee the design of the **Fasano Rio Hotel** (Av. Vieira Souto 80, Ipanema, tel. 21/3202-4000, www.fasano.com.br, R$1,560-2,100 d). With a team of Brazilian artists, the French design guru sought to conjure up the spell of 1950s Rio with a contemporary twist. The sea is prominently on display from the fabulous rooftop pool, fitness center, and spa as well as the sumptuous guest rooms—in the deluxe apartments, you can even see the ocean while taking a shower. Both the elegant **Al Mare** restaurant and the clubby **Baretto-Londra** bar are fervent fashionista hot spots.

Ruling the luxury roost of Leblon is Rio's "other" boutique hotel: the **Marina All-Suites** (Av. Delfim Moreira 696, Leblon, tel. 21/2172-1100, www.marinaallsuites.com.br, R$870-1,270 d). The 39 suites range from sizable to massive, and the beautiful decor is as personalized as the pampering you'll receive from the staff. The result is top-of-the-line comfort that is both refined and homelike, which explains the faithfulness of a classy celeb clientele (Gisele prefers the Diamante suite). Other model types can be seen hanging around the penthouse pool, taking in a film at the in-house movie theater, or downing caipirinhas at the enchanting **Bar d'Hotel.**

FOOD

Rio has an impressive restaurant scene featuring the best of so-called *alta* and *baixa culinária* (high and low cuisine). *Alta* cuisine has really taken off in Rio since the 1990s. The neighborhoods of Ipanema, Leblon, Jardim Botânico, and, to a lesser extent, Centro have seen a rise in stylish eateries owned and operated by some of the country's vanguard chefs. Meanwhile, many traditional neighborhood *churrascarias* and *botequins* offer up tasty *comida caseira* (home cooking) ranging from hearty *caldos* (soups), robust sandwiches, and barbecued chicken and beef to the classic Saturday *feijoada.*

Although carnivores fare well in Rio, seafood lovers will be equally spoiled. In keeping with Cariocas' fame as a body-conscious bunch, there are also numerous vegetarian, organic, and all-around healthy eateries—many of them self-service per-kilo buffets where diners can control their weight down to the last gram—particularly in the Zona Sul, where juice bars serve up dozens of varieties of fresh fruit juices, vitamin drinks, and healthy *sanduíches naturais.*

In recent times, a new crop of charming cafés has sprung up, many of them located in the city's cultural centers, cinemas, and *livrarias* (bookstores), where the desserts tend to be quite fabulous. As you'll witness everywhere from the street *barracas* in Lapa to the *padarias* (bakeries) in Copa, Cariocas have a pronounced sweet tooth, and satisfying sugar cravings is absurdly easy.

Although Rio's top restaurants are not cheap, it's definitely worth your while to splurge once or twice (also know that many offer more reasonably priced weekday *menus executivos* for lunch). You can then atone for your sins by seeking out more reasonably priced culinary experiences at the city's beach *barracas,* bars, bakeries, and bookstores.

Centro

You'll find a wide range of eating options in Rio's commercial hub, from speedy self-service buffets and bars serving *prato feitos*, or "PFs"—simple home-cooked specials of the day, usually consisting of the basic meat, beans, and rice triumvirate—to contemporary bistros, many located near the area's museums and cultural centers.

Botequins

Rio is legendary for its *botequins*, informal bars that function as neighborhood headquarters for residents from all walks of life. Whether considered *pé sujo* ("dirty foot," mildly mangy holes-in-the-wall) or *pé limpo* ("clean foot," somewhat more refined and upscale), the simple *botequim* is a democratic enclave where Cariocas get together to talk about *futebol*, politics, or their sex lives for hours at a time.

The drink of choice is an ice-cold *chope* (draft) served in traditional glasses that come in three sizes: the *tulipa* ("tulip"), the *garotinho* ("little boy"), and the rarely seen, mug-size *caldeireta* (Cariocas subscribe to the belief that the larger the glass, the warmer and more undrinkable the beer gets). There are always plenty of mouthwatering *petiscos* (bar snacks); the most common are *bolinhos de bacalhau* (deep-fried codfish balls), *carne seca desfiada* (shredded sun-dried beef), and velvety thick *caldo de feijão* (black bean broth), traditionally served with chopped cilantro, *torresmos* (pork rinds), lime, and *pimenta* (hot pepper).

CAFÉS AND SNACKS

★ **Confeitaria Colombo** (Rua Gonçalves Dias 32, tel. 21/2505-1500, www.confeitaria-colombo.com.br, 9am-8pm Mon.-Fri., 9am-5pm Sat.) is an exceptionally elegant belle epoque café, one of the few vestiges of how grand life must have been if you were an aristocrat in turn-of-the-20th-century Rio. More than a century later, Colombo is still a Rio institution: While working Cariocas cluster around the bar chasing pastries with *cafezinhos*, slack-jawed tourists can take *chá da tarde* (high tea) in the salon or indulge in the Saturday afternoon *feijoada*, accompanied by live samba and choro.

Ideally located in the foyer of the Centro do Comércio do Café (the 100-year-old regulating body of Brazil's prize crop), **Rubro Café** (Rua da Quitanda 191, tel. 21/2223-2265, www.rubrocafe.com.br, 7am-6pm Mon.-Fri.) is where the people who really *know* about coffee go to get their caffeine fix. More than 20 gourmet coffee drinks are served in this airy, modern space, as well as breakfast fare, sandwiches, salads, and desserts.

BISTROS AND LIGHT FARE

Looking out onto a whitewashed courtyard inside the Paço Imperial, **Bistrô do Paço** (Praça XV 48, tel. 21/2262-3613, www.bistro.com.br, 11:30am-7:30pm Mon.-Fri., noon-7pm Sat.-Sun., R$20-35) offers a tranquil oasis from the surrounding noise and traffic of Centro. Lunch is a rapid but tasteful affair with delicious salads, sandwiches, and daily specials.

Brasserie Rosário (Rua do Rosário 34, tel. 21/2518-3533, www.brasserierosario.com.br, 11am-9pm Mon.-Fri., 11am-6pm Sat., R$20-40) is a gourmet café, delicatessen, bakery, wine cellar, and bistro all rolled into one attractive, high-ceilinged, stone-walled building that once housed the Imperial Treasury. Happy-hour jazz and samba sessions at 6pm have a loyal following.

LOCAL COMFORT FOOD

With wooden shelves crammed to the ceiling with glittery bottles, **Paladino** (Rua Uruguaiana 224, tel. 21/2263-2094, 7am-8:30pm Mon.-Fri., 8am-noon Sat., R$15-25) is a quintessential Carioc *boteco* that's been around for more than a century. It's beloved by downtown workers for its cheap, home-cooked lunch specials, particularly omelets stuffed with *bacalhau* and shrimp.

SEAFOOD

Rio's oldest restaurant, **Rio Minho** (Rua do Ouvidor 10, tel. 21/2509-2338, 11am-3pm Mon.-Fri., R$40-55) hasn't changed much since it first opened its doors in 1884. The small traditional eatery is famed for its *sopa Leão Veloso*, a heady bouillabaisse-like stew of shrimp and fish heads flavored with leeks and cilantro. Owner Ramon Dominguez also owns Anexo next door, which serves smaller (and cheaper) portions.

Lapa

Lapa really comes into its own at night, which is also when you're more likely to find more appetizing sustenance. Bars are much more prevalent than restaurants, and they all serve *petiscos*. For a full-fledged meal, your best bet is to seek out traditional *botequins*. A good option is **Nova Capela** (Av. Mem de Sá 96, tel. 21/2252-6228, 11am-4am daily, R$20-35), the only one of Lapa's old-time *botequins* that stays open into the wee hours. Over the years it has become the classic pit stop after samba-ing the night away at Lapa's neighboring clubs and dance halls.

Santa Teresa

Santa's ongoing metamorphosis into an alternative arts *bairro* has spilled over into its restaurant scene, as local entrepreneurs, artists, and an increasing number of European expats are transforming century-old mini-palaces into gourmet eateries with bewitching views. Local residents often head to a handful of charming, decades-old *botecos* that continue to serve up *petiscos* and *comida caseira* at much more affordable prices.

CAFÉS AND SNACKS

From her home, **Alda Maria** (Rua Almirante Alexandrino 116, tel. 21/2232-1320, www.aldadocesportugueses.com.br, 2pm-7pm Tues.-Sun.) sells Portuguese sweets and pastries that she makes using recipes passed down by her grandmother. Cholesterol-phobics beware: Invented centuries ago in Portuguese convents, most of the pastries rely heavily on eggs (Alda Maria claims she cracks more than 800 a week).

At **Cafecito** (Rua Paschoal Carlos Magno 121, tel. 21/2221-9439, www.cafecito.com.br, 9am-10pm Sun.-Tues. and Thurs., 9am-11pm Fri.-Sat., R$15-35), one of Santa's inexplicably few cafes, the terrace—festooned with orchids and the occasional monkey—is a languorous place to relax. Options include

gourmet sandwiches, tapa-ish portions, and craft beers.

BRAZILIAN

Romantic and aptly named ★ **Rústico** (Rua Paschoal Carlos Magno 121, tel. 21/2221-9439, 1pm-10pm Sun.-Tues. and Thurs., 1pm-1am Fri.-Sat., R$25-45) is just up the stone steps from Cafecito's entrance. Sample creations such as grilled pineapple and brie salad, wild boar with baked apple, or *galinhada* (chicken stew with saffron rice served in a bubbling soapstone pot). Pizzas baked in a firewood oven are less adventurous but equally tasty. **Aprazível** (Rua Aprazível 62, tel. 21/2508-9174, www.aprazivel.com.br, noon-11pm Tues.-Sat., noon-6pm Sun., R$50-80)—the name is Portuguese for "delightful"—is the perfect name for this restaurant occupying a bucolic villa. Polished jacaranda tables spill out onto the veranda and lush tropical garden, which overlooks the Baía de Guanabara. The wine menu, designed by American expat and indie filmmaker Jonathan Nossiter, focuses on unsung local vintages. Reservations recommended.

Glória and Catete

Adega Portugália (Largo do Machado 30, Catete, tel. 21/2558-2821, 8am-midnight daily, R$20-35) is a friendly neighborhood restaurant-bar whose no-nonsense menu traffics in favorites such as grilled sardines and a legendary lamb risotto (served only on weekends), served in robust portions.

Flamengo and Laranjeiras

The most interesting eating options in this *bairro* are the handful of alluringly retro *botequins* and restaurants that have survived from the area's early 20th-century heyday.

CAFÉS AND SNACKS

Famed for its chocolate-covered carrot-cake, **Maya Café** (Rua Ortiz Monteiro 15, Laranjeiras, tel. 21/2205-4950, www.mayacafe.com.br, 9am-9:30pm daily) is a tranquil neighborhood nook that serves mouthwatering croissants, cakes, gourmet sandwiches, and salads as well as coffee. At night, caffeinated customers switch to wine and a delicious assortment of antipasti.

BRAZILIAN

Walking into ★ Tacacá do Norte (Rua Barão do Flamengo 35, Flamengo, tel. 21/2205-7545, 8:30am-11pm Mon.-Sat., 9am-9pm Sun., R$25-35) is like taking a trip to the Amazonian state of Pará. The standout is the namesake *tacacá,* a shrimp-filled broth flavored with *tucupi* (a yellow sauce made from wild manioc root) and *jambu* leaves, which leave your mouth tingling. Juices made from unpronounceable Amazonian fruits are ambrosial.

CHURRASCARIAS

The classic unfussy decor of Majórica (Rua Senador Vergueiro 11-15, Flamengo, tel. 21/2205-6820, noon-midnight Sun.-Thurs., noon-1am Fri.-Sat., R$40-60), where slabs of meat and a massive charcoal *churrasqueira* are prominent features, belie the fact that this is one of Rio's most traditional, and best, *churrascarias.* Traditional garnishes such as potato soufflé, french fries, *farofa* (toasted manioc flour) with eggs and banana, and *arroz maluco* ("crazy rice" that features bacon, parsley, and matchstick potatoes) are served separately. On weekends, avoid the immense family lineups by arriving after 3pm.

LOCAL COMFORT FOOD

At Lamas (Rua Marquês de Abrantes 18, Flamengo, tel. 21/2556-0799, www.cafelamas. com.br, 9:30am-2am Sun.-Thurs., 9:30am-4am Fri.-Sat., R$40-60), which originally opened in 1874, everything from the food and suave bow-tied waiters to the retro ambience is suffused with an aura of Rio's dining past. The food is honest, solid fare without surprises; try the famous filets mignons or the *filé à francesa,* served with matchstick potatoes and green peas flavored with diced ham and onions.

Botafogo, Cosme Velho, and Urca

These traditional residential neighborhoods are best known for their old *botequins* and Portuguese *tascas* that serve up tried-and-true *comida caseira,* but as Botafogo's nightlife has blossomed, so has the culinary scene.

CONTEMPORARY

With a name that's the Brazilian equivalent of "yum yum," Miam-Miam (Rua General Góes Monteiro 34, Botafogo, tel. 21/2244-0125, www.miammiam.com.br, 7pm-midnight Tues.-Fri., 8pm-1am Sat., R$35-45) is a tiny but very romantic café-bar owned and operated by Roberta Ciasca. At 21, Ciasca went backpacking through Europe and ended up at Paris's Cordon Bleu cooking school. In 2006, when she decided to convert her grandmother's turn-of-the-20th-century house into a restaurant, her creative comfort food—such as arugula rolls stuffed with roast beef and parmesan, or chicken pancakes with asparagus, mushrooms, emmental, and tarragon—quickly seduced the city's gourmets.

VEGETARIAN

Chácara is Portuguese for a rural estate, which is what it feels like when you arrive at Vegana Chácara (Rua Hans Staden 30, Botafogo, tel. 21/8599-7078, noon-3pm Mon.-Fri., R$20-30). Operated by two macrobiotic vegans who live on the second floor, the restaurant's daily options are so delicious that many carnivores stop by to savor meatless versions of Brazilian classics such as *feijoada* and *moqueca.* There's even a vegan caipirinha (the cachaça is replaced by ginger). Meals are paid for in cash, which you place in a box (make your own change).

Copacabana and Leme

Although the views from the tourist-flooded restaurants along Avenida Atlântica are incomparable, the food is usually overpriced and lackluster. Otherwise, Copa's most edible options are divided between the five-star kitchens of its most luxurious hotels and a few traditional restaurants and *botequins*.

CAFÉS AND SNACKS

Just around the corner from the Copacabana Palace, **La Fiducia Café** (Rua Duvivier 14, Copacabana, tel. 21/2295-7449, 7am-10pm daily) is a lively little café with sidewalk tables that make excellent perches for people-watching. Even if you have breakfast in your hotel, the pastries and coffee are so good you might want seconds. In the evening, it's a languorous spot for a glass of wine and a plate of pasta.

INTERNATIONAL

Considered by many to be Rio's top Japanese restaurant, **Azumi** (Rua Ministro Viveiros de Castro 127, Copacabana, tel. 21/2541-4294, 7pm-midnight Sun.-Thurs., 7pm-1am daily, R$35-75) emphasizes substance—and sushi—over style. Classic recipes are expertly prepared and presented in a pared-down, multilevel space. Slip off your shoes in one of the bamboo-screened rooms and Zen out before the check snaps you back to reality.

The ornate Middle Eastern trappings at **Amir** (Rua Ronald de Carvalho 55-C, Copacabana, tel. 21/2275-5596, www.amir-restaurante.com.br, noon-11pm Sun.-Fri., noon-midnight Sat., R$25-40) appear to be ripped out of a tale from *One Thousand and One Nights*. Despite the richness of the colors and fabrics on display, the Lebanese fare on Amir's menu is quite affordable, and portions are generous. A Leblon tentacle of Amir, **Yalla** (Rua Dias Ferreira 45, Leblon, tel. 21/2540-6517, www.yallabistro.com.br, noon-midnight daily, R$30) offers salads, shawarmas, falafels, and other light fare.

LOCAL COMFORT FOOD

The pioneer of the "favela-dining" phenomenon, the plastic chairs at ★ **Bar do David** (Ladeira Ary Barroso 66, Chapéu Mangueira, tel. 21/7808-2200, noon-5pm Tues.-Fri., noon-8pm Sat.-Sun., R$15-25) are as likely to seat local residents as Zona Sul foodies and foreign tourists. Owner David Vieira Bispo serves classic Brazilian homecooking with inventive twists. Pacific Chapéu Mangueira is just a quick, if steep, walk from Leme.

VEGETARIAN

Hidden in a little alley, **Naturaleve** (Rua Miguel Lemos 53, Loja B, Copacabana, tel. 21/2247-2900, 11am-8pm Mon.-Fri., 11am-4pm Sat., R$20-30) is a cheery, pistachio-green hole-in-the-wall. The vegetarian per-kilo restaurant serves a diverse selection of daily dishes as well as lots of organic, healthy goodies to go.

Ipanema and Leblon

The svelte and sun-kissed residents of these beach *bairros* dress up (casually chic) and go all out at international and contemporary restaurants, where the decor is as tasteful as the fare on the (usually pricey) menus. For lighter, more affordable sustenance, head to the neighborhoods' *botequins*, cafés, and delicatessens.

CAFÉS AND SNACKS

Armazém do Café (Rua Maria Quitéria 77, Ipanema, tel. 21/2522-5039, www.armazem-docafe.com.br, 8:30am-8:30pm Mon.-Fri., 8:30am-7pm Sat., 10am-6pm Sun.), a chain of gourmet cafés, currently has eight locations around Rio, including four in Ipanema. Armazém, which takes its beans quite seriously, is a great place to learn about and savor different Brazilian blends. For noshing, there are sandwiches as well as sweet and savory pastries.

Talho Capixaba (Av. Ataulfo de Paiva 1022, Loja A/B, Leblon, tel. 21/2512-8750, www.talhocapixaba.com.br, 7am-10pm daily) originally opened as a neighborhood butcher shop in the 1950s. Over the years it kept expanding, adding a fine-food delicatessen, a cheese shop, and one of the best bakeries in town. Choose from more than 20 types of bread and then design the sandwich of your dreams.

If you have a sweet tooth, you won't be able

to resist **Mil Frutas Café** (Rua Gárcia d'Avila 134, Ipanema, tel. 21/2521-1384, www.mil-frutas.com.br, 10:30am-12:30am Mon.-Fri., 9:30am-1:30am Sat.-Sun.), whose all-natural gourmet sorbets are made from native fruits such as *açai, bacuri, and cupuaçu*. Though there are not yet *mil* (1,000) flavors, there are close to 200. Although there are several locations around town, Ipanema's café also serves snacks and light meals.

BISTROS AND LIGHT FARE

A mere block from Ipanema beach, **Delírio Tropical** (Rua Gárcia d'Ávila 48, Ipanema, www.deliriotropical.com.br, tel. 21/3624-8164, 9am-9pm daily, R$20-35) is a great place for a healthy meal after soaking up the sun. Choose from an array of colorful and unusual salads along with hot daily specials, then take a seat in the upstairs dining area, where glass walls afford a tree house-like view of the comings and goings of beach below.

Tucked down a narrow alley from Ipanema's main drag, **Market Ipanema** (Rua Visconde de Pirajá 452, Ipanema, tel. 21/3283-1438, www.marketipanema.com.br, R$20-40) is a vibrant refuge. The décor is as fresh, light, and colorful as the healthy and tasty dishes, which appeal to both herbivores (red quinoa risotto) and carnivores (baby beef in a mustard-wine sauce). The caipirinha (made with passion fruit, lychees, strawberries, and basil) is wicked.

Located on the mezzanine of Ipanema's Livraria da Travessa, there's nothing at all bookish about sleek and sophisticated **Lado B** (Rua Visconde de Pirajá 572, Ipanema, tel. 21/2249-4977, www.bazzar.com.br, 10am-11pm Mon.-Fri., 9am-11pm Sat., noon-11pm Sun.). Serving breakfast, creative sandwiches, and bistro-style meals with Brazilian touches along with desserts, coffee, and drinks, it's an appealing place to hang out. Smaller versions are at Travessa branches in Shopping Leblon and Centro (Av. Rio Branco 44).

BRAZILIAN

Although Rio's most traditional dish—*feijoada*—is eaten on Saturday, **Brasileirinho**

(Rua Jangadeiros 10, Loja A, Ipanema, tel. 21/2513-5184, www.cozinhatipica.com.br, noon-11pm daily, R$25-40) has been serving up this quintessential stew for those (mainly gringos) who crave it any day of the week. The menu also traffics in succulent regional fare such as *carne seca com abóbora* (sun-dried beef with pumpkin) and *tutu à mineira,* a hearty stew of pork and pureed beans from Minas Gerais. The woodburning stove and rustic ambiance typical of the Interior décor comes as a refreshing shock.

CHURRASCARIAS

Son of Carioca superstar chef Claude Troisgros, Thomas Troisgros oversees the butchering and preparation of succulent meats at family-owned **CT Boucherie** (Rua Dias Ferreira 636, Leblon, tel. 21/2529-2329, www.ctboucherie.com.br, noon-4pm and 7pm-1am Mon.-Fri., noon-1am Sat.-Sun., R$60-90). Veggies and garnishes are given equal VIP treatment. An excellent wine list and contemporary decorative take on a classic French *boucherie* ensure an all-around appetizing experience.

CONTEMPORARY

Zaza Bistrô Tropical (Rua Joana Angêlica 40, Ipanema, tel. 21/2247-9101, www.zazabistro.com.br, 7:30pm-12:30am Mon.-Thurs., 7:30pm-12:30am Fri., 1:30pm-1:30am Sat., 12:30pm-6pm Sun., R$40-60) is a funky hippie-chic eatery where the organic and tropical (Asian, African, and American) rule. Red velvet flowers dangle from the ceiling of an upstairs room, where silk pillows litter the floor and shoes are optional. On the breezy, candlelit terrace, romance and relaxation are assured.

Foodie favorite **Zuka** (Rua Dias Ferreira 233, Loja B, Leblon, tel. 21/3205-7154, www.zuka.com.br, 7pm-1am Mon.-Fri., noon-4pm and 7pm-1am Sat., 1pm-midnight Sun., R$50-60) is presided over by Ludmila Soeira, one of Brazil's most exciting young contemporary chefs. Among her culinary fetishes is an old-fashioned charcoal grill; every hot dish passes over the grill's flames in some manner.

INTERNATIONAL

Spanish tapas are perfect for the Zona Sulistas' preoccupation with lithe figures and small portions. **Venga!** (Rua Dias Ferreira 113, Leblon, tel. 21/25129826, http://venga.com.br, 6pm-midnight Mon., noon-midnight Tues.-Wed. and Sun., noon-1am Thurs.-Sat., R$15-40) delivers with such aplomb that a second location opened in Ipanema (Rua Garcia D'Ávila 147b, 21/2247-0234, noon-1am daily). Tapas are as delectable as the people-watching from the terrace tables.

The penchant for small portions is so contagious that neighboring **Stuzzi** (Rua Dias Ferreira 48, Leblon, tel. 21/2274-4017, www.stuzzibar.com.br, 7pm-2am Mon.-Sat., 7pm-midnight Sun., R$28-38) jumped on the bandwagon—only in Italian. Rio is full of priccy *alta cocina* and pizza temples, but this subtle bar, with dim lighting and soft grey walls, is the real deal: Chef Paula Prandini did time at a Michelin-starred *ristorante* in Lombardy. The wine list focuses on Italian and Argentinian vintages.

The sushi chefs at **Sushi Leblon** (Rua Dias Ferreira 256, Leblon, tel. 21/2512-7830, noon-4pm and 7pm-1:30am Mon.-Wed., noon-1:30am Thurs.-Sat., 1pm-midnight Sun., R$50-75) are from the northeastern coastal state of Ceará, a region with a strong fishing tradition. Once they acquired Japanese preparation techniques, there was no stopping them—the sushi is sublime. While waiting for a table, do so in the company of a lychee caipisake (sake substitutes cachaça).

PER-KILO BUFFETS

Fellini (Rua General Urquiza 101, Leblon, tel. 21/2511-3600, www.fellini.com.br, 11:30am-4pm and 7:30pm-midnight Mon.-Fri., 11:30am-6pm and 7:30pm-midnight Sat.-Sun., R$25-40) offers one of Rio's most extensive and refined self-service buffets. There's no need to splurge at a five-star restaurant when you can savor the likes of lobster and escargots for a price only slightly higher than your average per-kilo joint. There are dishes for vegetarians and diabetics, and the dessert table is a world unto itself. On weekends, avoid prime time or you'll have to stand in line for some time.

One of Ipanema's organic pioneers, **New Natural** (Rua Barão da Torre 173, Ipanema, tel. 21/2287-0301, 7am-11pm daily, R$20-30) captures the healthy Zona Sul ethos to the hilt with offerings that appeal to both hard-core vegans and veggie-loving carnivores. The GLS community has claimed the place as a healthy hangout, and an onsite food store offers goodies to go.

VEGETARIAN

The tiny **Vegetariano Social Clube** (Rua Conde de Bernardote 26, Loja L, Leblon, tel. 21/2294-5200, www.vegetarianosocialclube.com.br, noon-midnight Mon.-Sat., noon-6pm Sun., R$20-25) opened when a group of health-conscious pals from Leblon decided to do something about the lack of hard-core vegan restaurants in the hood. Choose from buffet (lunch only) or à la carte options. To drink, there are lots of organic juices and even caipirinhas made with organic *cachaça* or sake. Sunday's tofu *feijoadas* (also served Wed.) have a large vegetarian following.

Lagoa and Jardim Botânico

The dozen sophisticated kiosks scattered around the Lagoa Rodrigo de Freitas offer a wide range of delicious fare, ranging from Arabian to Amazonian, both day and night. The reserved, upscale residential neighborhood of Jardim Botânico is second only to Ipanema and Leblon when it comes to gourmet eating experiences.

CAFÉS AND SNACKS

The lush tropicality of the Jardim Botânico became even more seductive with the opening of **La Bicyclette** (Rua Jardim Botânico 920, Jardim Botânico, www.labicyclette.com.br, tel. 3594-2589, 8:30am-9pm Mon.-Sat., 8:30am-4pm Sun.), a fetching French *boulangerie* that has become *le lieu* for flaky croissants, *pains au chocolat, croque monsieurs,* and gourmet sandwiches. The main location is nearby at Rua Pacheco Leão 320d.

Within the arcaded central courtyard of the Parque Lage are a sprinkling of tables that belong to ★ **D.R.I. Café** (Rua Jardim Botânico 414, Jardim Botânico, tel. 21/2226-8125, www.driculinaria.com.br, 9am-5pm daily), which offers an enticing selection of quiche, sandwiches, and pastries. Wines provide sustenance while you kick back and contemplate Christ the Redeemer's looming reflection in the courtyard's blue pool. Come on weekends for delicious brunch and live music.

INTERNATIONAL

One of Brazil's most stellar chefs, Claude Troisgros migrated from Paris to Rio 25 years ago and started a (culinary) revolution by marrying sophisticated French cooking techniques with Brazilian produce. You can savor Troisgros's original creations at ★ **Olympe** (Rua Custódio Serrão 62, Jardim Botânico, tel. 21/2537-6582, www.claudetroisgros.com.br, 7:30pm-12:30am Mon.-Sat., noon-4pm Fri., R$80-120). The restaurant's decor is as unpretentious and refined as the menus themselves (Troisgros offers several). Adventurous souls can splurge on the five-dish tasting feast (daily, R$260) that Troisgros dreams up according to the ingredients at hand.

INFORMATION AND SERVICES

Riotur (www.rioguiaoficial.com.br) is the city travel association. Pick up maps and brochures at its tourist centers as well as the excellent free *Rio Guide* (in English), with exhaustive listings, updated bimonthly. You can also consult the guide and even download it, along with city maps, from their website, and take advantage of its 24-hour tourist information hot line, Central 1746 (tel. 1746). The main center is in Centro (Praça Pio X 119, 9th Floor, tel. 21/2271-7048, 9am-6pm Mon.-Fri.). There are also branches in Copacabana (Av. Princesa Isabel 183, tel. 21/2541-7522,

9am-6pm, Mon.-Fri.) and at the Aeroporto Internacional Tom Jobim (7am-11pm daily). Small kiosks at various locations include Centro (Rua Candelária 6), Pão de Açúcar (Praça General Tibúrcio, Urca), and Ipanema (Rua Visconde de Pirajá at the corner of Rua Joana Angélica).

Exchange currency at **Banco do Brasil,** with branches at Aeroporto Internacional Tom Jobim, as well as in Centro (Rua Senador Dantas 105, tel. 21/3808-3900) and Copacabana (Av. Nossa Senhora da Copacabana 1292, tel. 21/3202-4400). The city has many ATMs; Banco do Brasil, HSBC, Bradesco, and Citibank also accept international bank cards. The largest concentrations of banks are on Avenida Rio Branco (Centro), Avenida Nossa Senhora da Copacabana (Copacabana), and Rua Visconde de Pirajá (Ipanema).

The main **post office** is in Centro (Rua 1 de Março 64), but there are branches at Aeroporto Internacional Tom Jobim (open 24 hours), in Copacabana (Av. Nossa Senhora de Copacabana 540), and in Ipanema (Rua Prudente de Morais 147). Hours are 8am-6pm Monday-Friday, 8am-noon Saturday.

Emergency Services

In the event of a medical emergency, dial **193** for Pronto Socorro (First Aid). If you need to visit a hospital in Copacabana, **Clínica Galdino Campos** (Av. Nossa Senhora de Copacabana 492, tel. 21/2548-9966, www.galdinocampos.com.br) is a private clinic that has a tradition of treating foreigners. It is open 24 hours and has English-speaking staff.

Rio is filled with pharmacies; many stay open 24 hours. Two 24-hour locations of **Drogaria Pacheco** are in Copacabana (Av. Nossa Senhora de Copacabana 534 A/B, tel. 21/2255-5222) and Catete (Largo do Machado 29, tel. 21/2205-8572).

In the event of a crime, call **190** to reach the police. There is a special **Delegacia Especial de Atendimento ao Turista** (Tourist Police) unit whose Leblon headquarters (Av. Afrânio de Melo Franco 159, tel. 21/2332-2924) is open

24 hours daily. Agents are generally helpful and speak English.

TRANSPORTATION

Most international travelers arrive in Rio by air, although if you're traveling from another city in Brazil, you'll likely arrive by bus or car.

Air

Rio has two airports. International flights and the majority of domestic flights arrive and depart from the **Aeroporto Internacional Tom Jobim** (Av. 20 de Janeiro, Ilha do Governador, tel. 21/3398-5050, www.aeroportogaleao.net). Also known as Galeão, it is in the Zona Norte, around 20 minutes from Centro and 45-60 minutes from Zona Sul. Right in Centro, adjacent to the Parque de Flamengo, is Rio's oldest airport, **Aeroporto Santos Dumont** (Praça Senador Salgado Filho, Centro, tel. 21/3814-7070, www.aeroportosantosdumont.net), where flights are basically limited to the Rio-São Paulo air shuttle.

Both airports have kiosks for special airport taxis, where you pay your fare in advance based on the distance of your destination. These are often more expensive (fare to Ipanema is R$105) than just hailing one of the yellow and blue *rádio taxis* available at the taxi stands (expect fare to Zona Sul to cost R$70-80). Make sure you use a bona fide taxi company, since there are a lot of "pirate" taxis. It should take around one hour to reach Ipanema, but if traffic is bad (as is frequently the case), it could take almost two.

From Galeão, the **Real** (www.realautoonibus.com.br) bus company offers regular *executivo* service for R$13.50 to Rio. Departing every 20 minutes between 5:30am-11:30pm, buses cut through Centro (along Av. Rio Branco) and then stop at Aeroporto Santos Dumont before continuing along the oceanfront *avenidas* of Flamengo (Av. Beira Mar), Copacabana (Av. Atlântica), Ipanema (Av. Vieira Souto), and Leblon (Av. Delfim Moreira) and then to Barra, including stops at all the major hotels along the way. For hotels that are inland, just ask the driver in advance

to let you off at the nearest cross street (*"Por favor, pode me deixar na Rua. . .?"*). To get to the airport, you can grab the same bus (on the reverse route) or ask your hotel to call you a cab and settle on a fixed rate in advance. Depending on the traffic, it can take between 90 minutes and two hours to reach Ipanema.

Bus

Close to Centro's port district, Rio's main bus station, **Rodoviária Novo Rio** (Av. Francisco Bicalho 1, São Cristóvão, tel. 21/3213-1800, www.transportal.com.br/rodoviaria-novo-rio), is a major transportation hub. Buses arrive from and depart to all points in Brazil and to other South American countries. Getting to and from the Rodoviária from anywhere in the city is easy. Just hop on any bus with "Rodoviária" posted as its destination on the front. A taxi will set you back around R$20 to Centro and R$40 to Copacabana. The area around the terminal is dodgy; exercise care.

MUNICIPAL BUS

Rio's municipal buses are not the safest form of locomotion due to pickpockets and occasional armed holdups. If you leave your valuables at the hotel and limit yourself to daytime trips between points in the Centro, Zona Sul, and the western beaches of Barra and Recreio, you'll be fine. Do take care to have your change already counted out beforehand, and always keep bags (including knapsacks) or other belongings closed (with a zipper or button) and close to your chest, especially when it's crowded. By day, buses run with great frequency. By night, you can risk taking buses between main stops in Flamengo, Botafogo, Copacabana, Ipanema, and Leblon, which are usually quite busy until around 9pm or 10pm. Otherwise, stick to taxis.

Final destinations are written on the front of the bus, and along the side are the main stops along the routes. Make sure you check this out. From Centro, for example, there are buses whose final destination is Leblon that careen along the coast through Copacabana and Ipanema, while others go inland via

Botafogo and Jardim Botânico. After paying your fare (R$3) to the *cobrador* at the back of the bus, make your way to the front, so you can make an easy exit when you get to your stop. If a bus stop is not clearly marked, look for a clump of people waiting. You can signal for a bus to stop by sticking out your arm.

Minibuses (or vans) have joined the traffic fray. They are often quicker for zipping between Centro and the Zona Sul since they can weave through traffic more easily. Destinations are listed on the windshield; fares hover between R$2.50-4.50.

Metrô

Rio's Metrô subway system (tel. 0800/595-1111, www.metrorio.com.br) is clean, efficient, and safe (and gloriously air-conditioned). The only problem is its size; spurred on by the 2014 World Cup and 2016 Olympic Games, Linha 1 is slowly expanding south, but currently it only goes to Ipanema/General Osório. Parts of the Zona Norte (Maracanã, for instance) and Centro are well served. In the meantime, MetrôRio has streamlined things considerably by adding "surface" Metrôs and express buses that depart from Metrô stations. For instance, to get from Ipanema to Leblon, Gávea, and Jardim Botânico, you can hop "subway buses" from Ipanema/General Osório station. From here, you can also transfer to a Barra Express bus. Express buses also leave from Largo do Machado, Botafogo, and Cardeal Arcoverde stations for Cosme Velho, Urca, and Leme, respectively. Tickets can be purchased in the stations. Fare is R$3.20, which includes a transfer to the "surface Metrô"; if transferring to an express bus, the fare for an *integração expressa* costs R$4.35. You can also purchase a prepaid Metrô card (the minimum charge is R$5) to which you can add as much credit as you want; not only is this cheaper than paying for individual fares, but you'll avoid lineups. The Metrô runs 5am-midnight Monday-Saturday, 7am-11pm Sunday. On weekends, you can board the trains with bikes and surfboards.

Taxis

Taxis are often the best way to get around Rio. Taxi service is reasonably priced, and for specific trips you can often bargain a fixed price with your driver (if language is a problem, ask someone at your hotel or hostel for help as well as approximate prices). There are two kinds of taxis in Rio. Yellow cabs with blue stripes are the most common. They can be hailed in the street and are cheaper. Large, white, air-conditioned radio cabs are usually ordered by phone and are more expensive. Two reliable companies are Central Táxi (tel. 21/2195-1000) and Coopacarioca (tel. 21/2518-1818). Most Carioca cab drivers are friendly and honest (although very few speak English), but there are a few who specialize in scamming gringo tourists. Unless you've agreed on a set fare, check to make sure the meter is always running. During daytime and until 8pm, the "Bandeira 1" rate is cheaper than at night and on holidays and weekends, when the rate is "Bandeira 2."

Car Rental

Driving in Rio de Janeiro is not exactly recommended. It's not that Cariocas are poor drivers, but they tend to forget they're not at the Indy 500. Then there are the rush-hour traffic jams, which are stressful and stiflingly hot. One-way streets, poorly marked turnoffs, and holdups—at stoplights and when you're parked—are further dissuading factors. In truth, renting a car only makes sense if you're going to be doing lots of day trips in and around the state of Rio de Janeiro. Major companies include Avis (www.avis.com.br), with agencies at Tom Jobim Airport (tel. 21/3398-5060) and Copacabana (Av. Princesa Isabel 350, tel. 21/2542-9937), and Localiza Rent a Car (www.localiza.com.br), with agencies at the Tom Jobim Airport (tel. 21/3398-5445), Santos Dumont Airport (tel. 21/2220-5604), Leme (Av. Princesa Isabel 150, tel. 21/2275-3340), and Barra (Av. das Américas 679, Loja C, tel. 21/2493-4477).

City Tours

An increasing number of organized tours allow you to explore Rio's diverse neighborhoods and natural attractions and to experience different aspects of Carioca life and culture.

Lisa Rio Tours (tel. 21/9894-6867, www.lisariotours.com, from R$120) is run by friendly, well-informed German expat Lisa Schnittger. Lisa offers a wide variety of tours in and around Rio including customized walking tours for individuals and small groups. Among her most popular outings are shopping in historic Centro, exploring Santa Teresa's bohemian life, and Afro-Brazilian culture in Rio.

Rio 4 Visitors (tel. 21/9355-9585, www.rio-4visitors.com) is run by multilingual Carioca native Daniel Cabral. Danny's car is comfy and air-conditioned and his enthusiasm is contagious whether he's introducing standard tourist attractions or little-known secret gems. Customized tours are based on the number of people, hours, days, and interests. He can pack a lot of Rio into one day.

Be a Local (tel. 21/9643-0366, www.bealocal.com) matches foreign visitors with English-speaking locals in an attempt to show them aspects of Carioca life—a funk party in a Rio *favela*, a soccer game at Maracanã—that they could never experience otherwise. A half-day trip with a *moto-boy* to a *favela* costs R$65.

Friendly British expat and foodie Tom Lemesurier gives **Eat Rio Food Tours** (http://eatrio.net/eat-rio-food-tours, email foodtours@eatrio.net), which combine historical and cultural anecdotes with walking and eating your way around the city.

Rio de Janeiro State

ILHA DE PAQUETÁ

Located in the Baía de Guanabara, the small Ilha de Paquetá (www.ilhadepaqueta.com.br) has been a favorite Carioca getaway since Dom João VI began coming here in the early 19th century. He was responsible for building the Capela de São Roque, around which the lively five-day **Festival de São Roque** takes place in August. On most weekends and holidays, the island is packed with families from the Zona Norte who crowd the seaside bars and (polluted) beaches (the cleanest are Moreninha, Imbuca, and José Bonifácio). During the week, though, the island offers splendid views of Rio and the bay and makes for a relaxing day trip. Tranquility reigns and the colonial buildings, although somewhat faded, retain their allure.

Transportation

Ferries leave at two-to-three hour intervals (5am-11pm daily) from the **Estação das Barcas** (tel. 0800/7211-0126, www.grupoccr.com.br/barcas, R$4.80) at Praça XV de Novembro. The trip takes a little over an hour. If you're in a hurry, hydrofoils (tel. 21/2533-4343) will get you there in half the time at double the price, with several departures and returns a day. Although no vehicles are allowed on the island, you can easily (and cheaply) rent a bike and pedal around.

NITERÓI

Only 17 kilometers (10.5 mi) across Baía de Guanabara, this well-to-do suburb-like city sports long white-sand beaches and space-age Niemeyer buildings, including the iconic *Star Trek*-worthy Museu de Arte Contemporânea.

Sights

The fantastic, UFO-shaped **Museu de Arte Contemporânea** (MAC; Mirante da Boa Viagem, Boa Viagem, tel. 21/2620-2400, www.macniteroi.com.br, 10am-6pm Tues.-Sun., R$4, free Wed.), designed by Oscar Niemeyer and inaugurated in 1996, sits on a slender cylindrical base of just 9 meters (30 feet). Since the museum overlooks the Baía de

Rio de Janeiro State

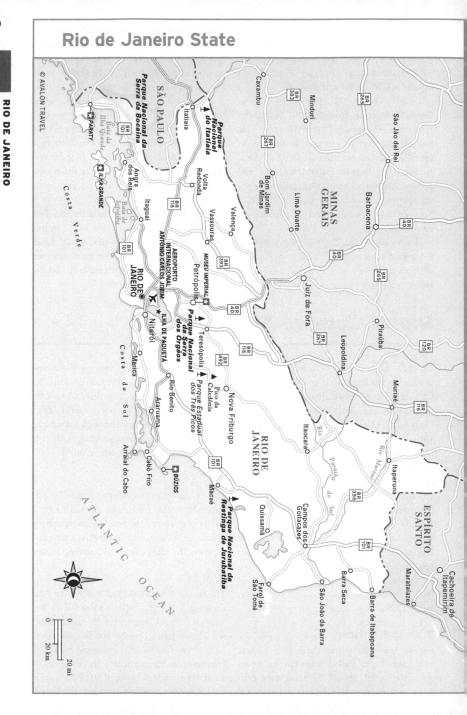

© AVALON TRAVEL

Guanabara, its 360-degree views are spectacular, often rivaling hit-or-miss art exhibits. To reach the museum from Niterói's ferry terminal, as you leave the terminal take a right and walk 50 meters (160 feet), then catch the 47B minibus.

The MAC was the first construction of the Caminho Niemeyer (Niemeyer Route). Other projects include the striking Teatro Popular and the Fundação Oscar Niemeyer. When (and if) completed, Niterói will be second only to Brasília as a showcase for the vanguard architect's constructions.

Beaches

The beaches close to Niterói's center are polluted, but take a bus due south—from the ferry terminal, any bus marked Itacoatiara—to encounter some surprisingly unspoiled and very attractive beaches, among them **Piratininga, Camboinhas, Itaipu,** and the most spectacular of them all, **Itacoatiara,** about 45 minutes from Niterói's center. From here, you have unrivaled views of Pão de Açúcar and Corcovado across the bay. All are well equipped with *barracas* where you can feast on fresh fish and seafood.

Transportation and Services

The municipal tourist office, **Neltour** (tel. 0800/282-7755, www.nitcroiturismo.com.br), has several information kiosks, including one at the ferry terminal and another at the Mirador Boa Viagem, the lookout point adjacent to MAC (both open 9am-6pm daily).

Although you can take a bus or drive across the Ponte Rio-Niterói, one of the world's longest bridges, the most scenic way to get to Niterói is by taking the ferry that leaves from the Estação das Barcas at Praça XV de Novembro. Boats operated by **Barcas S.A.** (tel. 0800/7211-0126, www.grupoccr.com.br/barcas)—often jammed with commuters during rush hour—leave at 15-30-minute intervals 7:30am-midnight and at 60-minute intervals midnight-6am. Ferry rides take 20 minutes. In Niterói, ferries and catamarans either dock at the Estação Niterói in the center

of town (fare is R$4.80) or at the Estação Hidroviária at Charitas (R$13).

PETRÓPOLIS

When the going gets hot, Cariocas have historically headed for the cool, forest-clad mountains surrounding Rio, where charmingly rustic resort towns conjure up a tropical version of the Alps. Only an hour's drive north from Rio, the summer getaway of the Brazilian emperor and his family provides a welcome refuge, offering cool respite, fine food, and mountain scenery. Upon discovering this idyllic region, Dom Pedro I was so enchanted by the majestic landscapes and moderate temperatures that he drew up plans for a villa. However, it fell to his son, Pedro II—who founded Petrópolis (named after his imperialness) in 1843—to actually build his dream house, which ended up as a full-fledged royal palace. Not wanting to be out of the loop, barons, counts, and marquises came flocking. The town's alpine climes also attracted numerous German immigrants, which explains the Bohemian influence present in the architecture and cuisine.

Exploring Petrópolis by foot is easy, but if you're feeling lazy, romantic, or both, hire a horse-drawn carriage (R$50 for up to five, 45 min.), available in front of the Museu Imperial. Having a car, while not essential, is a bonus, since you can easily go zooming off to nearby towns and take in a fuller range of natural attractions. Many appealing (and luxurious) lodges are hidden in beautifully remote spots, as are gourmet restaurants.

Sights

Most of historic Petrópolis lies beyond the somewhat congested commercial center, concentrated in a bucolic cluster of streets lined with 19th-century mansions and laced with tree-shaded canals. Many of the most splendid *casas* are on the main street of Avenida Koeler.

★ MUSEU IMPERIAL
Amid landscaped gardens, the elegant neoclassical pink edifice that served as Dom

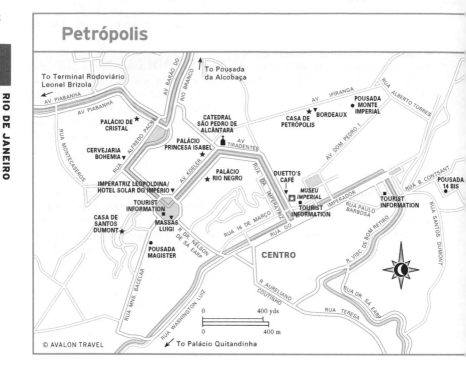

Pedro II's summer digs now houses the **Museu Imperial** (Rua da Imperatriz 220, tel. 24/2245-5550, www.museuimperial.gov. br, 11am-5:30pm Tues.-Sun., R$8). After replacing your shoes with soft-soled slippers, you can glide around the gleaming parquet floors and inspect the myriad regal trappings, whose highlights include Dom Pedro I's golden scepter and Dom Pedro II's fairy tale-like crown, encrusted with 639 diamonds and 77 pearls. The palace offers a rare day-in-the-life glimpse of an emperor in the tropics.

CATEDRAL DE SÃO PEDRO DE ALCÂNTARA

The imposing French neo-Gothic **Catedral de São Pedro de Alcântara** (Rua São Pedro de Alcântara 60, tel. 24/2242-4300, 8am-6pm daily), with its 70-meter (230-foot) tower (you can climb to the top—169 stairs—for R$8), wasn't completed until 1939. Its somber aura exterior houses lovely stained-glass windows, depicting scenes from poems written by the multitalented Dom Pedro II; the main attraction here is the marble, bronze, and onyx Imperial Mausoleum housing containing the mortal remains of Dom Pedro II, his wife, Dona Teresa Cristina, and their daughter, Princesa Isabel.

CASA DE SANTOS DUMONT

Brazilians have long snubbed their noses at the Wright Brothers. As far as they're concerned, the first human being to take to the skies in a plane was Alberto Santos Dumont, who in 1906 completed the first nonassisted flight in his plane, which he baptized *14-Bis*. Flying machines aside, Santos Dumont was an avid builder and inventor. He designed the gracious house known as **Casa de Santos Dumont** (Rua do Encanto 22, tel. 24/2247-3158, 9:30am-5pm Tues.-Sun., R$5). The house displays personal effects and various other inventions, among them an alcohol-heated shower and a bed that can be transformed into a desk.

PALÁCIO QUITANDINHA

Slightly outside of the center, most easily reached by car or taxi, the **Palácio Quitandinha** (Av. Joaquim Rola 2, tel. 24/2245-2020, 9am-6pm Tues.-Sat., 9am-5pm Sun., R$6) was built in the 1940s to house the largest and most glamorous hotel-casino in all of Latin America. While it attracted the likes of Marlene Dietrich, Orson Welles, and Lana Turner, its days as a luxury gaming den were short-lived; in 1946 gambling was outlawed in Brazil, and the casino was transformed into a posh apartment complex. Today, it functions as an SESC events center. You can explore its surprisingly vibrant interior—the work of famed American decorator and Hollywood set designer Dorothy Draper, who irreverently colored the walls in tones of shocking pink, scarlet, and turquoise, reminiscent of a Technicolor movie. Note that the lagoon out front is shaped like Brazil.

CASA DE PETRÓPOLIS

The former home of José Tavares Guerra, nephew of the Barão de Mauá (one Brazil's most famous entrepreneurs, he founded the Banco do Brasil), the **Casa de Petrópolis** (Rua Ipiranga 716, tel. 24/2231-8718, 1pm-6pm Fri.-Sun. and daily Jan. and July, R$8) is a Victorian mansion whose architecture was inspired by Guerra's early years spent living and studying in England. Guided tours are offered; the lovely gardens were a favorite strolling spot of Dom Pedro II.

Other Petrópolis palaces of note aren't open to visitors, but their exteriors are worth a look. These include the pretty pink **Palácio Princesa Isabel** (Av. Koeler, 42), home of the imperial princess, and the grand **Palácio Rio Negro** (Av. Koeler, 255), built by the Barão do Rio Negro, a rich coffee planter. After he sold it, the house became the official summer residence of Brazil's presidents. The **Casa do Barão de Mauá** (Praça da Confluência 3) was home to the Barão de Mauá.

Accommodations

There are a handful of basic accommodation options in Petrópolis's commercial center, as well as several nice hotels in the older, residential neighborhoods. An even larger number of *pousadas*—often quite posh and set in the midst of gorgeous landscapes—are located in the surrounding mountains, but you'll need a car to reach them. Sunday-Thursday, rates can be 20-50 percent lower.

Pousada 14 Bis (Rua Buenos Aires 192, tel. 24/2231-0946, www.pousada14bis.com.br, R$170-250 d), named after Santos Dumont's historic plane, is centrally situated and fetchingly rustic to boot. The lounge pays homage to the homegrown aviator-inventor with a smattering of engaging artifacts related to his life and times. Rooms are cozy and comfortable. Occupying an attractive European-style manor built in 1814, **Pousada Magister** (Rua Monsenhor Bacelar 71, tel. 24/2242-1054, www.pousadamagister.com.br, R$230-250 d) is in the midst of all of Petrópolis's historic attractions. The comfortable rooms lack much of a decorative scheme, but all boast soaring ceilings, immense windows, and polished wood floors. A steep uphill walk from the center of town, the **Pousada Monte Imperial** (Rua José de Alencar 27, tel. 24/2237-1664, www.pousadamonteimperial.com.br, R$215-370 d) is worth the physical exertion. With friendly service and compact, cozy rooms offering views of the town below, this *pousada* is an enchanting rural retreat within spitting distance of Petrópolis proper.

Surrounded by mansions that once belonged to barons and counts, **Hotel Solar do Império** (Av. Koeler 376, tel. 24/2103-3000, www.solardoimperio.com.br, R$440-700 d) will make you feel quite regal. This ornate 1875 mansion provided refuge for Princesa Isabel while her own *palácio* down the street was undergoing renovation. Stately rooms offer modern conveniences, and there's a swimming pool and a spa. The hotel's well-regarded restaurant, **Imperatriz Leopoldina** (7:30am-10pm Sun.-Thurs., 7:30am-midnight Fri.-Sat., R$40-70), specializes in elegantly presented dishes that draw on both European and Brazilian influences.

Food

Petrópolis is something of a gourmet destination, but many of the finest area restaurants are located along the Estrada União-Indústria, which winds from the Centro through the rural districts of Corrêas, Araras, and Itaipav—far from the city center and requiring a car. One of the best is ★ **Pousada da Alcobaça** (Rua Agostinho Goulão 298, Estrada do Bonfim, tel. 24/2221-1240, www.pousadaalcobaca.com.br, noon-10pm daily, R$45-65), located in the bucolic region of Corrêas (11 km, or 7 mi, from the center of Petrópolis, heading toward the Parque Nacional Serra dos Órgãos). This charming *pousada* occupies an early 20th-century Norman country house, surrounded by fragrant herb and vegetable gardens that supply produce for the excellent breakfasts, lunches, and teas prepared by 84-year-old owner and chef Laura Góes. Reservations are a must. You can also stay in exquisitely furnished comfortable rooms (R$385-550 d) occupying the main house or mill house.

In Centro and occupying a lovely old house with vaulted ceilings, **Massas Luigi** (Praça da Liberdade 185, tel. 24/2244-4444, www.massaluigi.com.br, 11am-midnight daily, R$20-35) is a fine place to go for tasty homemade pasta and pizzas. For a light meal or snack in imperial surroundings, the Museu Imperial's **Duetto's Café** (Av. Imperatriz 220, tel. 24/2243-2952, www.bistroimperatriz.com.br, 10am-6pm Sun. and Tues.-Wed., 10am-10pm Thurs.-Sat., R$15-25) is a great option, with a few entrées, salads, and sweet and savory pastries. In an irresistible setting in the shadow of the Casa de Petrópolis, **Bordeaux** (Rua Ipiranga 716, tel. 24/2242-5711, www.bordeauxvinhos.com.br, noon-midnight Mon.-Sat., noon-7pm Sun., R$15-25) is an emporium and bistro with delicious beers and wines to wash down nicely priced appetizers and gourmet sandwiches.

Beer lovers should head to the headquarters of **Cervejaria Bohemia** (Rua Alfredo Pachá 166, tel. 24/2247-5222, www.bohemia.com.br), home of Brazil's first beer. Considered one of Brazil's most quaffable brews (Pedro II was a fan), Bohemia was invented by a German immigrant who arrived in Petrópolis in 1853 and used the pure mountain water to craft this pale lager. In 2012, the historic brewery was transformed into a beer research center and **museum** (11am-6pm, Wed.-Fri., 11pm-8pm Sat.-Sun., R$20). At the adjacent **Boteco Bohemia** (tel. 24/3064-9127, noon-10pm Wed.-Thurs. noon-midnight Fri.-Sun.), sample the wares along with bar snacks that harmonize with individual labels.

Transportation and Services

Petrotur (tel. 0800/024-1516, http://destinopetropolis.com.br) operates several kiosks throughout town, including at Praça da Liberdade (9am-6pm daily) and across from the Museu Imperial (Praça Visconde de Mauá 305, 9am-6:30pm daily).

From Rio's Rodoviário Novo, **Única-Fácil** (tel. 0800/886-1000, www.unica-facil.com.br, 90 min., R$21) buses depart every 30 minutes from 5:30am-midnight to Petrópolis's long distance **Terminal Rodoviário Leonel Brizola** (tel. 24/2249-9856). From here, connect to a local bus (no. 100) to get to the downtown Terminal de Integração station in Centro (R$2.85) or take a cab (R$30). Buses leave approximately every 15 minutes. By car from Rio, take BR-040, which offers a splendid, if hair-raising, hour-long drive through the mountains; beware of rain and crowded weekend rush hours.

PARQUE NACIONAL DA SERRA DOS ÓRGÃOS

Created in 1939, **Parque Nacional da Serra dos Órgãos** (8am-5pm daily, R$25) owes its name to early Portuguese explorers, who thought that its strangely shaped rocky peaks bore an uncanny resemblance to a church pipe organ. Stretching between Petrópolis and Teresópolis, the park comprises 12,000 hectares (30,000 acres) of exuberant Atlantic forest with waterfalls, hiking trails, and the postcard-worthy **Dedo de Deus** (Finger of God), rising 1,692 meters (5,551 feet) above sea level. Higher but less dramatic is the **Pedra do Sino** (Bell Rock, 2,263 meters/7,425 feet). There are plenty of other peaks to marvel at and even scale—from the uppermost summits, on a clear day you can see all the way to Rio de Janeiro and the Baía de Guanabara.

The park is 5 kilometers (3 mi) from the center of Teresópolis on BR-116 leading to Rio. The entrance close to Petrópolis is 16 kilometers (10 mi) from the center of town on the Estrada União-Indústria.

Hiking

Numerous trails range from easy strolls to taxing but spectacular multiday treks. Since most trails are unmarked, hire a guide if you're thinking of doing more than a short hike. Guide information is available online and at the park's main entrance and headquarters in **Teresópolis** (Av. Rotariana, tel. 21/2152-1100, www.icmbio.gov.br/parnaserradosorgaos). There is also an entrance from **Petrópolis** (tel. 24/2236-0475). Entrance fees allow access to easier trails in the lower reaches of the park. For trails higher up the mountain, the fee is R$40 for the first day; an additional fee is charged on weekdays (R$4) and weekends (R$20). The longest and most challenging hike is the spectacular three-day trek between Petrópolis and Teresópolis (42 km/26 mi); consider starting from Petrópolis to get the hardest part out of the way first. Most guides charge around R$200 pp. For longer hikes and excursions such as rappelling and canyoneering, contact **Trekking Petrópolis** (tel. 24/2235-7607, www.rioserra.com.br/trekking). May-October is the best time for trekking; barring rain, November-February is more conducive to bathing in the park's many icy streams and waterfalls.

TERESÓPOLIS

Nowhere near as charming nor as imperial as Petrópolis, Teresópolis is a modern, upscale alpine resort whose name pays homage to Empress Teresa Cristina, wife of Dom Pedro II, who was taken by the area's magnificent mountain scenery and refreshing climate. Its main attraction lies in its proximity to the Parque Nacional da Serra dos Órgãos.

Accommodations and Food

Most of Teresópolis's worthy accommodations are tucked amid the mountains. The **Hotel Rosa dos Ventos** (RJ-130 Km 22.5 to Nova Friburgo, tel. 21/2644-9900, www.hotelrosadosventos.com.br, R$520-760 d) offers rustic yet luxuriously accessorized chalets with fireplaces and balconies. Nature lovers need never leave the hotel complex, which includes countless walking and biking trails, two swimming pools, a lake for kayaking, and stables for horseback riding. Also on the premises are three gourmet restaurants (full-board rates are higher) and an English bar.

More central and much cheaper is the **Várzea Palace Hotel** (Rua Prefeito Sebastião Teixeira 41, tel. 21/2742-0878, hotelvarzea@bol.com.br, R$65-125 d). Although its early 20th-century elegance has faded, this formerly grand hotel offers clean and comfortable rooms with sky-high ceilings, parquet floors, and lots of retro character.

Manjericão (Rua Flávio Bortoluzzi de Sousa 314, Alto, tel. 21/2642-4242, 6pm-11pm Thurs.-Fri., noon-midnight Sat., noon-11pm Sun., R$25-35) serves a delicious thin-crust pizza baked to perfection in a wood-burning oven. Herbs and vegetables come from the restaurant's garden.

Transportation and Services

For maps and information about the surrounding area, head to the centrally located **tourist office** (Praça Olímpica, tel. 21/2742-5661, 8am-6pm daily) or visit www.teresopolis.rj.gov.br (in Portuguese).

Viação Teresópolis (tel. 21/2742-0606, ww.viacaoteresopolis.com.br) offers hourly bus service from 6am-10pm between Teresópolis and Rio de Janeiro (2 hours, R$27) and every 2-3 hours between Teresópolis and Petrópolis (2 hours, R$17). The bus station is close to the central main square. To reach Teresópolis directly from Rio by car (1.5 hours), take BR-040 and BR-116. The driving time by car between Petrópolis and Teresópolis is about 45 minutes.

NOVA FRIBURGO

Although it's hard to imagine, in the early 1800s Switzerland was so (temporarily) poor that 100 Swiss families left their hometown of Fribourg to settle in these mountainous climes. This explains the prevalence of wooden chalets, chocolate shops, and restaurants serving cheese fondue and raclette here, one of Brazil's oldest and only Swiss colonies. What it doesn't explain: Nova Friburgo is the Brazilian capital of lingerie. In the downtown *bairros* of Olaria and Ponte da Saudade (near the bus station), dozens of fine lingerie manufacturers export nationally and throughout the world, and discriminating shoppers can pick up fancy underthings for a song.

To survey the surrounding countryside, from the Alto do Cascatinha neighborhood (accessible via local bus to "Cascatinha-Interpass," R$3) take a steep but gratifying 6-kilometer (3.5-mi) hike up to the 2,310-meter (7,579-foot) summit of **Pico da Caledônia**; the top provides breathtaking views and also serves as a launching pad for hang gliders.

Within close proximity is the **Parque Estadual dos Três Picos** (Estrada do Jequitibá 145, Cachoeiras de Macacu, tel. 21/2649-5847, www.inea.rj.gov.br, 9am-4:30pm daily, free), Rio de Janeiro's largest state park. Easy trails are near the entrance; for more ambitious treks and climbs, a guide is required. Serious mountain climbers will want to hike to the top of the *três picos* (three peaks)—the two loftiest, Pico Maior and Montanha do Capacete (which measures 2,316 meters/7,598 feet), can only be scaled with climbing gear. Entrance to the park is at Km 46.5 on RJ-130 going to Teresópolis. At the entrance is the Refúgio da Águas, where you can contract a guide.

Accommodations and Food

In Centro, **Hotel São Paulo** (Rua Monsenhor Miranda 41, tel. 22/2523-5984, www.hotelsaopaulo.com.br, R$180 d) is a simple yet atmospheric 1940s hotel with original fixtures and details that cast a vintage spell, although the décor veers toward Spartan.

If you want to be surrounded by mountain greenery, there are multiple options in the surrounding area. One of the nicest is **Hotel Akaskay** (Estrada Eduardo Francisco do Canto 643, RJ-116 Km. 71.5, Mury, tel. 22/2542-1163, www.akaskay.com, R$280-320 d), some 8 kilometers (5 mi) from Friburgo. Owned by a landscaper and conservationist, the grounds are beautiful, as are the cozy wood cabins built from reforested wood and outfitted with quilts and fireplaces. A natural swimming pool, walking trails, and waterfalls ensure you never have to leave the property.

One of Friburgo's finest and most centrally located restaurants, the petite and charming ★ **Crescente Gastronomia** (Rua General Osório 21, tel. 22/2523-4616, www.crescenterestaurante.com.br, 11:30am-11pm Mon. and Thurs.-Sat., 11:30am-5pm Sun., R$40-70) has an eclectic, French-inflected menu. For cheaper, heartier fare, try **Dona Mariquinha** (Rua Monsenhor Miranda 110, tel. 22/2522-2309, noon-3:30pm Tues.-Sun., 7pm-9pm Mon.-Fri., R$35 pp). This 50-year-old institution specializes in homecooked Brazilian comfort food, which does the rounds of the dining room *rodízio* style in an all-you-can-eat rotating buffet.

Transportation and Services

The **tourist office** (Praça Doutro Demervel B. Moreira, tel. 22/2543-6307, www.pmnf.rj.gov.br/turismo, 8am-8pm daily) has maps and hotel listings as well as information about hikes and walks. **Viação 1001** (tel. 21/2516-3797, www.autoviacao1001.com.br) has hourly departures from Rio's Rodoviária Novo to Nova Friburgo via Niterói (3 hours, R$36-45) from 5am-11pm. Buses arrive at the Rodoviária Sul (Ponte de Saudade), 4 kilometers (2.5 mi) south of the center of town. If you're coming from Teresópolis via **Viação Teresópolis** (tel. 21/2742-0606, www.viacaoteresopolis.com.br, 2 hours, R$18, five daily departures), you'll arrive at the

Rodoviária Norte (Praça Feliano Costa), about 2 kilometers (1.2 mi) north from the center. If you're driving from Rio, you'll need to head across the Rio-Niterói bridge and then follow BR-101, BR-104, and BR-116.

PARQUE NACIONAL DO ITATIAIA

Brazil's oldest national park, **Parque Nacional do Itatiaia** (tel. 24/3352-1292, www4.icmbio.gov.br/parna_itatiaia, 8am-5pm daily, R$25 for foreign visitors), founded in 1937, spans the state frontiers of Rio de Janeiro, São Paulo, and Minas Gerais. The easily accessible lower regions are covered with lush native Atlantic forest, wild orchids, and begonias, and spectacular waterfalls such as **Itaporani, Véu de Noiva,** and **Maromba,** all of which are easy to reach and boast beckoning (if chilly) pools for bathing. Numerous easy hiking trails can be easily explored by families, without a guide, and are readily accessible from the pretty mountain towns of **Itatiaia** and **Penedo.** The upper part of the park—dominated by a stark and imposing landscape of sculpted rocks—also has its attractions, among them the dramatic peaks of **Agulhas Negras** (2,548 meters/8,360 feet) and **Prateleira** (2,791 meters/9,157 feet). To scale them, you'll have to be in superb shape and be accompanied by a guide (consult the park's website for a list). Prices for hikes on the lower portion cost around R$60 pp, while scaling Prateleira and Agulhas Negras is R$120 pp (group rates are cheaper).

The entrance to the lower portion of the park is easily reached by following the 5-kilometer (3-mi) stretch of BR-116 that links the town of Itatiaia to the park entrance. This is where you'll find the visitors center, which offers information and maps. The upper portion of the park is accessed via the town of Itamonte in Minas Gerais, 65 kilometers (40 mi) from Itatiaia. The best times to visit the lower parts of the park are January-February and October-December, when it's warmer for bathing. For climbing Agulhas Negras and Prateleira, May-August is better due to the clear skies and low rainfall (although temperatures can get chilly).

Accommodations and Food

The town of **Itatiaia** is the best and most convenient base for visiting the park. Its many hotels are located on BR-116, which leads to the park's entrance. **Chalés Terra Nova** (Estrada Parque Nacional, Km 4.5, tel. 24/3352-1458, www.chalesterranova.com.br, R$240-290 d, full board) offers basic but comfortable accommodations split between a main house and individual chalets, which are ideal for groups or families. Amenities include a sauna, swimming pool, a small lake for trout fishing, a treetop walking course, and mountain bikes for pedaling around. The oldest and one of the finest hotels in the region, **Hotel Donati** (Estrada Parque Nacional, Km 9.5, tel. 24/3352-1110, www.hoteldonati.com.br, R$295-415 d full board) is located within the park itself. Since 1931, its charm-laden chalets have sheltered nature lovers, including composer and poet Vinicius de Moraes and modernist painter Alberto da Veiga Guignard (who was inspired to paint the doors and windows of the main cabin). Some chalets have jetted tubs; all have fireplaces. Among the restaurant's many offerings are fresh trout and fondues.

Sabor de Itatiaia (Estrada Parque Nacional, Km 3, tel. 24/3352-3050, 11:30am-3:30pm Mon., 11:30am-3:30pm and 7pm-11pm Tues.-Fri., 11:30am-11pm Sat.-Sun., R$20-30) is a per-kilo buffet featuring hearty fare bubbling over a wood burning stove. On weekends *churrasco* joins in the offerings, and at night the oven turns out piping hot pizzas.

Transportation and Services

For information about Itatiaia, visit the **tourist office** (Praça Mariana Leão Rocha 20, tel. 24/3352-6777, 10am-6pm daily, closed off-season). **Cidade do Aço** (tel. 0800/886-1000, www.cidadedoaco.net) operates seven daily departures from Rio's Rodoviária Novo to Itatiaia (2.5 hours, R$35). By car from Rio, take BR-116.

Costa do Sol

Running east from Rio, the Costa do Sol lives up to its name by offering more than 100 kilometers (60 mi) of gorgeous coastline. In summertime, the main towns of Cabo Frio, Arraial do Cabo, and Búzios come alive with activity.

ARRAIAL DO CABO

Arraial do Cabo is only 6 kilometers (4 mi) south of overdeveloped Cabo Frio, yet this fishing port town is more tranquil than either Cabo or frenetically fashionable Búzios to the south. The crystalline waters off Arraial are a diver's paradise, and Praia de Farol, on nearby Ilha de Cabo Frio, is considered one of the most beautiful beaches in Brazil.

Beaches

Closest to town is **Praia dos Anjos,** an attractive strip of sand with enticing turquoise waters whose only flaw is that it can get a little packed with water-sports enthusiasts. In 1503, Amerigo Vespucci landed on these sands (a plaque above the beach marks the spot) and was so taken with the spot that he left 24 of his cohorts behind to start a colony. It's only a short walk to the beaches of **Prainha** (north of town) and the sweeping stretch of **Praia Grande** (to the west)—equipped with *barracas* serving fresh fish and seafood—that extends all the way up to the Brazilian surfers' paradise of Saquarema. You can also follow a steep 1-kilometer (0.6-mi) trail from Praia dos Anjos (or take a boat) to the lovely and deserted **Praia do Forno,** where you can snorkel and then relax at a floating restaurant-bar. **Praia do Pontal** is another exceptional beach whose calm waters are backed by small dunes and native vegetation. The 4-kilometer (2.5-mi) walk from Arraial involves a steep climb up the Morro do Atalaia; at the top, catch sight of migrating humpback whales in the winter. An alternative is to take a boat.

The most fantastic beach, **Praia do Farol,** is on Ilha do Farol, a sublime island paradise fringed with fine white sand and sculpted dunes, whose 390-meter (1,280-foot) peak offers magnificent views. Praia do Farol has been scientifically classified as "the most perfect beach in Brazil." Unfortunately, you won't be able to stay long: since the Navy controls the island, you can only spend a maximum of one (pre-authorized) hour basking on its shores. Most boat excursions (with the necessary permission) stop here.

Diving

Arraial is considered one of the best spots for recreational diving in Brazil. Its transparent blue waters are the only place where the ocean currents (which usually flow north-south along the Brazilian coast) flow east-west, provoking a phenomenon whereby the deep, cold currents from Antarctica rise to the surface. While this means that water temperatures are always quite cold, it also results in the presence of many nutrients, which in turn attract an unusually rich variety of marine life. Add to this more than 30 sunken galleons—the consequence of heavy pirate activity off the coast during the 17th and 18th centuries—and you're in for an underwater treat.

An outing, including equipment rental and a snack, should cost around R$160. For more information, contact **PL Divers** (tel. 22/2622-1033, www.pldivers.com.br) or **Arraial Sub** (Av. Getúlio Vargas 93, tel. 22/2622-1945, www.arraialsub.net).

Boat Excursions

A wonderful way to explore Arraial's marine splendors is by boat. **Arraial Tur** (Rua Dom Pedro II, 02 A, Praia dos Anjos, tel. 22/2622-1340, http://arraialtur.com.br) offers three-hour schooner excursions for R$40, with stops at the beaches of Pontal do Atalaia and Ilha do Farol. On the island, you can visit Gruta Azul,

Costa do Sol

an underwater cavern that turns blue when illuminated by the sun.

Accommodations and Food

For cheap digs, it's hard to beat the pleasant **Hostel Marina dos Anjos** (Rua Bernardo Lens 145, Praia dos Anjos, tel. 22/2622-4060, www.marinadosanjos.com.br, R$160-185 d, R$55-65 pp). Dorm rooms are spotless if a little overpriced, as are double, triple, and quadruple rooms. Common rooms (including a well-equipped kitchen) have a more appealing, loungey beach house vibe; Praia dos Anjos is conveniently close, and an obliging staff is full of regional information. You can also rent bikes and diving equipment. Located on a quiet little street near the pier, family-owned **Pousada Canto da Baleia** (Rua Kioto 30, Praia dos Anjos, tel. 22/2622-1156, www.cantodabaleia.com.br, R$325-400 d) offers sunny and modern accommodations with attentive service. A small pool, plenty of hammocks, and the possibility of a home-cooked meal make this a great choice. **Pousada Pilar**

(Rua Sérgio Martins 27, Praia dos Anjos, tel. 22/2622-1922, www.pousadadopilar.com.br, R$220-260 d) is a bit like staying in a tropical antiques store; the owners' taste for found objects and artworks mingle with salvaged materials and lush plants. Rooms are large and attractive, and the common spaces—pool, gardens, solarium, kitchen—are inviting.

Portuguese expat Tuga spent years hawking his legendarily crunchy *bolinhhos de bacalhau* before opening his own restaurant, **Bacalhau do Tuga** (Praia dos Anjos, tel. 22/2262-1108, 6pm-11pm Wed.-Fri., 1pm-11pm Sat.-Sun., R$20-35). The *pastéis de nata* (Portuguese custard tarts) are sublime. Al fresco tables and a dining room adorned with Asterix and Obelisk frescos are at French-run **Saint Tropez** (Praça Daniel Barretto 2, Praia dos Anjos, tel. 22/2262-1222, 6pm-midnight Mon.-Tues., noon-midnight Wed.-Sun., R$25-40). Along with very decent pizza at night, the local daily catch is served up in a diverse array of succulent dishes incorporating fresh fish, shrimp, squid, and mussels.

Transportation and Services

Located at the entrance to town, the **tourist office** (tel. 22/2262-1949, www.arraial.rj.com. br, 8am-5pm daily) has information about excursions as well as diving and boating trips. **Viação 1001** (tel. 21/2516-3597, www.autoviacao1001.com.br) has departures every 1-2 hours, 5am-11pm, from Rio's Rodoviária Novo to Cabo Frio via Niterói. The 2.5-hour journey costs R$59. The *rodoviária* (Praça da Bandeira) is in the center of town.

★ BÚZIOS

Búzios is the Gisele Bündchen of Brazilian beach resorts: internationally renowned, naturally beautiful, sophisticatedly chic. Before it became Brazil's most stylish beach getaway, Armação de Búzios was a tiny fishing village perched on the tip of a peninsula, 190 kilometers (118 mi) east of Rio de Janeiro. All of that changed in 1964, when sultry French starlet Brigitte Bardot happened upon it with her Brazilian boyfriend of the moment. Aided by the international paparazzi, the bikinied "B. B." singlehandedly put the place on the map. Before long, she had moved on to other boys and other beaches, but idyllic Búzios—the name by which both the village of Armação and the entire peninsula came to be known—quickly became a favorite stop on the global jet-setters' paradise party circuit.

Búzios's narrow cobblestoned streets, yacht-infested waters, and softly illuminated, cactus-studded landscapes are decidedly Mediterranean. As the little town has grown, both the permanent population and the tourists who flock here every summer are increasingly global and moneyed. Although the cachet of its Bardot days is long gone, those prepared to fork out big bucks will also gain a very considerable bonus: unlimited access to some of Brazil's most enchanting beaches. Time your visit to avoid the summer months, and you'll find a more pleasantly placid Búzios and a considerably more affordable one as well.

The peninsula of Búzios has three main settlements. Closest to the mainland on the isthmus, Manguinhos is the most commercial; from here, the principal thoroughfare of Avenida José Ribeiro Dantas cuts straight through the peninsula, morphing into the Estrada Usina Nova as it arrives in the village of Armação dos Búzios. The touristy and hedonistic center of Búzios, Armação clusters chic boutiques, hotels, restaurants, and night spots along the celebrated main drag of Rua das Pedras and its extension, the Orla Bardot. A 15-minute walk north along the coast from Armação brings you to the peninsula's oldest settlement, Ossos (the name "Bones" hints at its early whaling days), whose pretty harbor continues to charm.

Beaches

Visitors to Búzios may either take or leave its cosmopolitan trappings, but no one can resist its beaches. There are 24 of them, ranging in size from tiny isolated coves to mile-long sweeps of sand, each flaunting its own distinctive attributes and personality.

The beaches closest to the northern part of the isthmus at Manguinhos are Praia de Manguinhos and Praia Rasa, where high winds and low waves attract windsurfers and sailboats as well as families with kids. Going toward Armação, Praia dos Amores and Praia das Virgens are unspoiled, quite deserted, and framed by lush vegetation. Praia da Tartaruga's limpid blue waters are

Praia da Armação, Búzios

the warmest on the peninsula and ideal for snorkeling.

While the beaches in Armação—**Praia do Canto** and **Praia da Armação**—are pretty to contemplate, they are too polluted for swimming. Picturesque **Praia dos Ossos** attracts sailors and windsurfers but also isn't recommended for bathing. Farther north, the tiny twin (and surprisingly primitive, if you arrive early) beaches of **Azeda** and **Azedinha** are framed by exuberant foliage and famed for their unofficial topless sunbathing. The clear blue waters are good for snorkeling, as are those of neighboring **João Fernandes** and **João Fernandinho.** Long and wide, trendy João Fernandes is framed by dozens of beach bars that serve fresh lobster and seafood. João Fernandinho is smaller and less crowded, with enticing natural pools for bathing.

On the easternmost tip of the peninsula lie wilder, windswept, and isolated beaches—reached by car or by following offshoots of the Estrada Usina Velha. With rugged cliffs and stormy seas, **Praia Brava** impresses with rosy pink sand and rough swells that attract surfers. **Praia Olho de Boi** is a seductive little cove favored by nudists, while **Praia do Forno** and **Praia da Foca** are picturesque and tranquil, their calm blue waters set off by rocks decorated with twisting cacti.

On the southern end of the peninsula, going toward the mainland, **Praia da Ferradura** consists of a large *ferradura* (horseshoe) bay ringed with mansions, condos, *pousadas*, and bars. Its protected waters are popular with families as well as fans of sailing and windsurfing. Pretty **Praia da Ferradurinha**'s transparent waters are good for diving.

Closest to the mainland, **Praia de Geribá** is a long, sweeping beach that is beautiful but quite urbanized. It's usually flooded with surfer boys and partying twentysomethings lured by electronic beats emanating from multiple beach *barracas*. Much more rustic and unspoiled are **Praia dos Tucuns, Praia José Gonçalves,** and **Praia das Caravelas,** all accessible via the road leading to Cabo Frio.

You can reach most beaches by municipal bus (R$2). Taxis and minivans regularly careen up and down the peninsula via Avenida José Ribeiro Dantas/Estrada Usina Nova. By day, *taxis marítimos* (R$5-20) shuttle passengers to and from the northern peninsula beaches from piers at Armação and Praia dos Ossos.

Diving

The limpid blue waters off the peninsula offer ideal conditions for diving. **Casamar** (Rua das Pedras 242, Armação, tel. 22/2623-8165, www.casamar.com.br) organizes daily excursions that include snacks and drinks for divers of all levels (as well as lessons) to the islands of Âncora and Gravatá, where you can see bright coral and fish, sea turtles, and, if you're lucky, dolphins. A four-hour beginner's course costs R$220, and a morning excursion with two tanks and equipment, R$160; it's also possible to rent snorkels, masks, and fins (R$25).

Sailing, Windsurfing, and Kite Surfing

The wind conditions at many of Búzios's beaches are excellent for sailing and windsurfing. **Búzios Vela Clube** (Praia de Manguinhos, tel. 22/2623-0508) offers lessons as well as equipment rental. Eight hours of windsurfing and sailing lessons cost around R$600 pp. Equipment rental costs R$50 (sailboats) and R$50 (windsurf board) per hour. Praia Rasa has become a mecca for aficionados of kite surfing. **Búzios Kitesurf School** (tel. 22/9956-0668, www.kitenews.com.br) offers lessons and rents equipment; a basic 8- to 10-hour course costs R$1,500.

Boat Excursions

Interbúzios (tel. 22/2623-6454, www.interbuzios.com) offers daily three-hour schooner trips (R$40 pp), with various departure times, that stop at 12 beaches and three islands. More rapid and more frequently booked are the daily catamaran excursions (R$60 pp) offered by **Tour Shop** (tel. 22/2623-4733, www.tourshop.com.br), which hit 15 beaches and four islands and provide snorkels and masks as well as drinks. Both depart from the pier at Praia de Armação.

Nightlife

Búzios's nightlife is concentrated along Armação's Rua das Pedras and Avenida José Bento Ribeiro Dantas. Whie the nocturnal scene fizzles off-season, during the summer months it boils over. Things don't get going until around 11pm, and the partying, which entails a lot of eating, drinking, and checking people out, is so intense that most of the area's hotels serve breakfast until noon and most boutiques don't open their doors until the afternoon.

Búzios institution **Chez Michou** (Rua das Pedras 90, tel. 21/2623-2169, www.chezmichou.com.br, noon-close daily) is famous for its mouthwatering crepes; choose from more than 40 sweet and savory fillings. At night, it becomes one of Búzios's major hot spots, as does **Pátio Havana** (Rua das Pedras 101, tel. 22/2623-2169, 6pm-close Thurs.-Sun., daily in summer), a sophisticated place with a whiskey club, bistro, tobacco shop, and stage that hosts live jazz, blues, and MPB performers. Once you've warmed up, it's time to dance the night away. **Pacha** (Rua das Pedras, tel. 22/2633-0592, www.pachabuzios.com, 10pm-7am Fri.-Sat., daily in summer) prides itself on importing top international DJs, while **Privilège** (Orla Bardot, tel. 22/2620-8585, www.privilegenet.com.br, 8pm-close Thurs.-Sun., daily in summer) is where you can work up a sweat, chill out on the terrace, or ramble its five bars (one serves sushi). Some clubs go into hibernation off-season.

Accommodations

To be near all the action in Búzios, stay in Armação or Geribá; if you prize tranquility and seclusion, consider accommodations at the peninsula's other beaches. Búzios is definitely not a bargain, especially in high season, when reservations are a must. If you choose to come during the off-season (anytime other than July and Dec.-Mar.) or during

the week, you can take advantage of discounts of up to 30-40 percent. The lower-priced options are small but homey *pousadas* in and around Armação and Ossos. Prices listed are off-season.

Located just off Praia de Geribá, **Marésia de Búzios Guest House** (Rua das Pitangueiras 12, Bosque de Geribá, tel. 22/2623-3876, www.maresiadebuzios.com.br, R$150-170 d, R$50-60 pp) is a hostel that feels more like a B&B. Rooms are in a gleaming white beach-style house with living rooms and shady lawns for sprawling or barbecueing. A quartet of private doubles have small patios.

Owned and operated by a charming French couple, **L'Escale Pousada Restaurant** (Travessa Santana 14, Praia dos Ossos, tel. 22/2623-2816, www.pousadalescale.com, R$160-220 d) offers simple but fetching rooms in a cozy house overlooking the placid Bay of Ossos. The nicest rooms sport terraces with picturesque sea views, and the main floor is occupied by a bistro.

Immersed in nature but only a stone's throw from Rua das Pedras, **Villa Balthazar** (Rua Maria Joaquina 375, Praia da Ferradura, tel. 22/2623-6680, www.villabalthazar.com.br, R$345 d) offers five lavish private rooms that mingle vintage and modern furnishings with flawless panache and attention to detail. A lounge, library, herb-scented garden, and small pool are invitations to unwind while nursing cocktails and listening to birdsong from the adjacent lake.

Checking into ★ **Casa Búzios** (Alta do Humaitá 1, Praia da Armação, tel. 22/2623-7002, www.pousadacasabuzios.com, R$300-540 d) is like visiting a friend's rambling, sunny beach house (albeit a friend with impeccable taste); each of the thematically decorated rooms has its own charismatic personality. Dining, drinking, and lounging take place in the charming main house surrounded by patios, gardens, and a pool with views toward the sea.

Casas Brancas Boutique Hotel & Spa (Alto do Humaitá 10, Praia da Armação, tel. 22/2623-1458, www.casasbrancas.com.br,

R$680-1610 d) has been around since 1973, long before the term *boutique hotel* had been uttered. The cluster of Andalusian-like white hilltop *casas* overlooking Praia da Armação possess none of the contrived sleekness of more contemporary design hotels. Yoga classes and treatments are offered at the on-site spa, and a delightful terrace restaurant serves up Brazilian-Mediterranean fare.

Cachoeira is Portuguese for waterfall, and at Cachoeira Inn (R. E1, Lote 18, Praia da Ferradura, tel. 22/2623-2118, http://cachoeirainnbuzios.com, R$880-1,700 d), nine waterfalls wind their way down ingeniously landscaped cliffs to the blue waters of Ferradura Bay. The four luxurious suites are each named after a world-famous waterfall.

Food

Among the excellent and budget-saving per-kilo buffet palaces along Rua Manuel Turíbia, Bananaland (Rua Manuel Turíbia de Farias 50, Centro, tel. 22/2623-2666, www.restaurantebananaland.com.br, 11am-11pm daily, R$20-30) is the most charming and healthy. The more anonymously palatial Buzin (Rua Manuel Turíbia de Farias 273, Centro, http://buzinbuzios.com, tel. 22/2623-7051, 11:30am-11pm daily, R$20-30) offers greater diversity and a little more bang for your buck.

The Orla Bardot concentrates some of Búzios' most sophisticated and celebrated restaurants, all with romantic views of the sea. One of the most adventurous is Salt (Orla Bardot 468, Praia da Armação, tel. 22/2623-2691, www.restaurantesalt.com.br, 5pm-midnight Sun.-Thurs., 5pm-3am Fri.-Sat., R$65-80). The contemporary menu, conceived by Ricardo Ramos Ferreira (an able disciple of French superchef Alain Ducasse), draws upon global influences from Italian risottos and Moroccan couscous to Thai red curries. Bucking Orla's trendy (and pricey) eateries is O Barco (Orla Bardot 1054, Praia da Armação, tel. 22/2629-8307, 6pm-close daily Dec.-Feb., Tues.-Sun. Mar.-Nov., R$60-75).

Terrace and sidewalk tables are perfectly positioned for savoring generous portions while watching the sunset.

João Fernandes, Brava, Ferradura, and Geribá have idyllic palm-thatched bars that serve up grilled fish and seafood at reasonable prices. At Fishbone Café (Av. Gravatás 1196, Praia de Geribá, tel. 22/2623-7348, http://fishbonebuzios.com, 11am-5pm daily, R$25-45), you can enjoy salads and sandwiches. More secluded and clubby is the idyllic cliffside ★ Rocka Beach Lounge (Praia Brava, tel. 22/2623-6159, www.rockafishfish.com.br, 11am-5pm daily, R$40-60), where you can sink your teeth into fish and seafood delicacies while sprawling in lounge chairs and sofas.

Transportation and Services

A tourist office is just off the main square of Praça Santos Dumont in Armação (Travessia dos Pescadorees 151, Centro, tel. 22/2623-2099, www.visitebuzios.com, 8am-10pm daily). A good source of online information is the bilingual website www.buziosonline.com.

Búzios is a little more than two hours by car from Rio. Viação 1001 (tel. 21/2516-3597, www.autoviacao1001.com.br) operates almost hourly daily buses (3 hours, R$47) between 6am-9:30pm from Rio's Rodoviária Novo to Búzios. Buses arrive at the virtually nonexistent Búzios Rodoviária (Estrada da Usina Nova 444, tel. 22/2623-2050), which is only a few minutes' walk from the Orla Bardot. By car, after crossing the Rio-Niterói bridge, turn onto BR-101 leading to Rio Bonito. Close to Rio Bonito, turn onto RJ-124 before turning onto RJ-106, which leads to Búzios. The journey is close to 200 kilometers (125 mi) and should take around two hours. Another alternative is to hitch a ride in an air-conditioned minivan. Búzios-based Malizia Tour (tel. 22/2623-1226, www.maliziatour.com.br) offers transportation between Rio and Búzios with pickup and deposit at your hotel or the airport for R$90 pp.

Costa Verde

Stretching south from Rio de Janeiro to the state of São Paulo, Costa Verde (Green Coast) is one of southern Brazil's most captivating and (for the time being) unspoiled coastlines.

★ ILHA GRANDE

Only 160 kilometers (100 mi) south of Rio, the port town of Angra dos Reis anchors a magnificent bay whose aquatic realm embraces 1,000 beaches and (supposedly) 365 islands. The largest, Ilha Grande, boasts more than 100 pristine beaches, including the breathtaking *praias* of **Lopes Mendes, Cachadaço, Saco do Céu, Aventureiro,** and **Parnaioca.** A 90-minute boat ride from Angra, Ilha Grande's 192 square kilometers (74 square mi) are entirely preserved and offer abundant walking trails and a wide range of accommodations.

Before becoming one of Brazilians' retreats from civilization, Ilha Grande went through phases as a pirate hangout and a leper colony. It also housed two penitentiaries, reserved for some of Brazil's most hardened and violent criminals. Although the second prison was demolished in 1994, opening the door to tourism, the not-yet-overgrown ruins of the original jail still cast a slightly haunting spell.

No motorized vehicles are allowed on the island. Ferries and launches all dock at the main village of **Vila do Abraão,** a picturesque, palmy, beachfront settlement of 3,000 people (the population swells in the summer months). Vila do Abraão, with its cobblestone streets and pastel-hued houses, provides the main base for exploring—on foot or by boat—the island's natural attractions.

Beaches

An hour's walk south of Vila do Abraão brings you to **Praia Grande das Palmas,** a tiny fishing village in the shade of a forest of swaying palms. Another 40 minutes away, the palms give way to mangroves at **Praia dos Mangues.** Despite the loveliness of both, most earnest beach pilgrims are loath to linger when they know that a mere 20-minute walk will bring them to **Praia Lopes Mendes,** considered by many to be the most beautiful beach in all of Brazil. Walking along its 3-km (2-mi) expanse, the shimmering bands of emerald and indigo sea are unearthly. To savor it by yourself, head toward the left, where you can relax in the shade of an almond tree; to the right is surfer central, where *surfistas* can rent boards and take lessons. The immaculate state of Lopes Mendes is guaranteed by its limited access: boats aren't allowed to dock in its inlet. Visitors who are loathe to hike from Vila do Abraão must catch one of three daily boats that shuttle between town and Praia dos Mangues (45 min.), then continue on by foot.

Further afield is **Cachadaço,** a small but shimmery jewel of a beach whose size (15 meters, 50 feet) is compensated for by a secluded setting of dramatic boulders and rain forest. Invisible from the open sea, it was a favorite pirate refuge. Divers can climb the rocks and plunge into the emerald pool below. To get here from Abrãao takes more than three hours on foot, two hours by boat.

A two-hour trek south from town along an old prison road leads to **Praia dos Dois Rios,** whose sands are bracketed by *dois rios* (two rivers). The rain forest behind the beach, near the village of Dois Rios, camouflages the vestiges of the Cândido Mendes penal colony. The small **Museu do Cárcere** (tel. 24/2334-0939, 10am-4pm Tues.-Sun.) pays homage to its checkered past. Among its illustrious captives were 20th-century novelist Graciliano Ramos, who wrote about his experience in the classic *Mémorias do Cárcere,* and legendary Lapa *malandro,* Madame Satã, who spent 16 years here for killing a policeman.

Far more remote (6 hours on foot from Abrãao) is **Praia da Parnaioca,** where the Rio Parnaioca creates a freshwater lagoon that offers a sweet alternative to saltwater bathing. On the western end of the south coast, the unspoiled allure of **Praia do Aventureiro** stems from its location within a nature reserve (although it can be reached on foot and by boat). During periods when the waves swell to heights of 4 meters (13 feet), it becomes a surfers' paradise.

Diving and Boat Excursions

The best way to discover Ilha Grande's beaches, coves, and grottoes is by boat. **Ilha Grande Turismo** (tel. 24/3361-6426, www.ilhagrandeturismo.com.br) offers full- and half-day trips on large schooners (with 70 passengers, free-flowing caipirinhas, and pulsing musical soundtracks, R$30-50 pp for 6 hours) as well as on smaller, faster motorized launches for up to 20 people (R$120-180 pp for 6-8 hours). Trips usually include visits to 7-8 beaches with stops for snorkeling, diving, basking in the sun, and lunch. You can also hire a *táxi-boat* at the **Associação dos Barqueiros de Ilha Grande** (tel. 24/3361-5046, R$30-50 pp).

Elite Dive Center (tel. 24/3361-5501, www.elitedivecenter.com.br) offers lessons, equipment rental, and diving excursions to the most scenic underwater spots around the island. A beginner's course (R$200) includes a six-hour excursion with a 45-minute dive; a more intensive four-day course (R$960) includes five dives.

Rain Forest Hikes

Enthusiasts can tap into their inner Tarzan or Jane by tackling the numerous hiking trails that weave through the island. The rain forest is home to a variety of wildlife, including monkeys, parrots, hummingbirds, and (unfortunately) many mosquitoes—for your sanity, repellent is a *must*. Most trails are well signed, but it's best to take a few precautions, such as informing your *pousada* of your route and equipping yourself with water, snacks, and sunscreen. Also carry a flashlight, since night can fall quickly.

One of the easiest walks from town is along the road that leads to **Lazareto** (20 min.), the site of the late 19th-century hospital where leprosy and cholera patients were quarantined. Towering over the ruins is a 26-arch aqueduct that supplied the hospital with water. At one end of the aqueduct is a smooth, chair-shaped stone where Emperor Pedro II often sat to compose poetry and sketch. From the aqueduct, a 90-minute walk along a rain forest trail leads to the Cachoeira da Feiticeira, a

Praia Lopes Mendes

15-meter (50-foot) waterfall that plunges into natural pools fit for bathing. Since the trail is poorly marked, hire a guide.

For serious treks into the interior, such as the five-hour hike across the island to Praia da Parnaioca or the three-hour climb up to the summit of Pico do Papagaio (Parrot's Peak), it's wise to hire a guide (R$80). Ilha Grande Turismo organizes day trips (R$160 pp) as well as overnight camping and hiking excursions led by bilingual guides.

Accommodations

Most accommodations are located in or around Vila do Abraão, although some more exclusive *pousadas* are hidden in secluded natural settings. Camping sites abound, while *pousadas* tend to be fairly simple, although not always cheap.

There's no shortage of hostels in Ilha Grande, but small, tidy, and modern Biergarten (Av. Getúlio Vargas 153, tel. 24/3361-5583, http://biergartenhostel. blogspot.com, R$130 d, R$60-90 pp) is one of the nicest. Lots of exposed red brick and wood, along with bright colors, make it more homey than hostel-y. There are two communal kitchens; an on-site restaurant (lunch and dinner) mixes a mean cocktail and serves a cheap, delicious, and vegetarian per-kilo buffet.

At ★ Pousada Naturália (Rua da Praia 149, tel. 24/3361-5198, www.pousadanaturalia.net, R$170-210 d), double, triple, and quadruple suites are handsomely finished with polished natural wood and wide terraces where you can settle into a hammock and gaze out to sea. Cozy Pousada Mara e Claude (Rua da Praia 333, tel. 24/3361-5922, http://ilhagrande.org/maraeclaude, R$180-220 d) looks right onto the beach. The friendly French proprietors have decorated the modest guest rooms with homey touches that will make you feel like a prized houseguest.

The trump card at Pousada Aratinga (Rua das Flores 232, tel. 24/3361-9559, www. aratingailhagrande.com.br, R$280-350 d) is hands-on hostess and Scottish transplant

Rennie, who is responsible for everything from the guest rooms' homey touches to the scrumptious cakes that accompany afternoon tea. A small pool and hammocks increase the relaxation factor, as does distance from the Vila's madding crowd. Set into a hillside overlooking the sea, the sprawling rooms at Pousada Asalem (Praia da Crena, tel. 24/3361-5602, www.asalem.com.br, R$460-580 d) offer maximum comfort and Edenic isolation, despite being only a 25-minute walk (or 15-minute boat ride) from town. If you feel stranded, hop into a complimentary kayak or canoe and contemplate your own private seascape.

Food

Vila do Abraão has lots of simple, rustic bar-restaurants to choose from. Dom Mario (Travessa Buganville, tel. 24/3361-5349, open Mon.-Sat., R$20-30) is a nicely priced favorite. Local chef Mario gets fancy with fresh seafood, yielding generously portioned creative fare such as octopus Provençal and fish doused in passion-fruit sauce. Lua e Mar (Rua da Praia 297, tel. 24/3361-5113, 11am-10pm Thurs.-Tues., R$25-45) provides tables and chairs spread out beneath a giant tree overlooking the beach. Located in the beach-front *pousada* of the same name, O Pescador (Rua da Praia, tel. 24/3361-5111, 5pm-11pm Mon.-Sat., R$50-70) offers tasty and inventive dishes, such as shrimp with leeks and gratiné pineapple, along with a small but well-chosen wine menu.

Information

Ilha Grande's tourist office (Rua da Praia, tel. 24/3367-7826, 7am-7pm daily) is located close to where the ferries dock. Nearby, the Centro de Visitante do Parque Estadual (Av. Beira Mar, tel. 24/3361-5540, 8am-5pm daily) has maps and information regarding the natural park covering much of the island. The bilingual website http://visiteangradosreis.com.br and the Portuguese www.ilhagrande.com and www.ilhagrande.org also have information about the area. There are no vehicles on Ilha Grande, nor bank machines—come equipped with cash (although many places accept credit cards). Internet service is sketchy to nonexistent in many places.

Transportation

Ilha Grande can be reached by boat via three towns along the Costa Verde: Angra dos Reis, Mangaratiba, and Conceição de Jacareí. **Viação Costa Verde** (tel. 21/3622-3123, www.costaverdetransportes.com.br) offers hourly bus service between 4am-9pm from Rio's Rodoviária Nova to Angra (3 hours, R$44); six daily buses to Conceição de Jacareí (2.5 hours, R$37) and four to Mangaratiba (2 hours, $R31). Angra-bound buses can also drop you in Conceição, if you ask the driver to do so. The advantage of going to Conceição is that the most frequent number of scheduled boats depart from here; speedboats (R$30, 25 mins.) and schooners (R$20, 45 min.) leave every 1-2 hours between 9am-6pm. Angra and Mangaratiba are the departure points for the cheaper but less frequent regular ferries operated by **CCR Barcas** (tel. 0800-721-1012, www.groupccr.com.br/barcas, R$4.80, 80 min. from both ports). Ferries depart from Angra 3:30pm weekdays and 1:30pm weekends and from Mangaratiba at 8am daily, with an extra ferry at 10pm Friday. **Ilha Grande Turismo** (tel. 24/3365-6426, www.ilhagrandeturismo.com.br) also operates speedboats from Angra to Ilha Grande (R$30, 45 min.) with departures at 8am, 11am, and 4pm. Tickets can be purchased at Angra's bus station.

A door-to-door shuttle service can save time and transfers. **Easy Transfer** (tel. 21/9386-3919, www.easytransferbrazil.com) operates vans that pick you up at your hotel in Rio and take you all the way to Ilha Grande (R$80, 4 hours). By car, follow the BR-101 (the Rio-Santos highway) to Angra, where you can leave your car in a parking area. Beware of weekend traffic.

★ PARATY

In the early 1700s, the Portuguese were looking for ways to transport gold found in neighboring Minas Gerais across the ocean and into their coffers. Traders widened an ancient Guaianá Indian trail that led through the Serra do Mar mountain range and down to the sea; at the end of the route sprouted the tiny port town of Paraty. Over the next few decades, Paraty grew into a modest yet stately town, its cobblestoned streets filled with single-story whitewashed mansions and austere but elegant churches. Yet it remained an isolated spot that was difficult to defend. Increasing bandit raids and pirate attacks took their toll and led to the building of a new gold route that linked Minas's gold towns directly with Rio de Janeiro.

As a consequence, Paraty's importance declined, and over the next two centuries the town, always remote, slowly fell into oblivion. Its faded architecture remained frozen in time, preserved by its very isolation. It wasn't until 1960 that the town was connected to both Rio de Janeiro and São Paulo by BR-101, the Rio-Santos highway. Shortly afterward, in 1966, its historic center was declared a national monument, and in the 1970s, Paraty began to attract a small trickle of hippies and artists drawn to its bucolic vibe and rich historic legacy. Artists and entrepreneurs transformed its 18th- and 19th-century houses, which in turn lured a steady stream of weekenders from Rio and São Paulo as well as international tourists and, more recently, an alternative GLS crowd.

In the summer and during July, Paraty can get quite busy, but so far it has managed to stave off hysteria and trendiness. During the off-season, the town is languorous without being dull, and it is easier to soak up its seductive atmosphere. Within close proximity are dozens of gorgeously primitive beaches and deserted islands, along with the majestic Serra do Mar mountain range.

Sights

Paraty's compact *centro histórico* is considered by UNESCO to be one of the world's outstanding examples of Portuguese colonial architecture. Although the streets are laid out on a grid plan, the uniformity of the bleached houses coupled with streets' multiple names can make it somewhat of a challenge to find your bearings. The crazily paved streets—constructed by slaves out of large irregular stones known as *pés-de-moleque* ("street kids' feet")—mean that vehicles can't circulate, but also make getting around treacherous for those with disabilities or sporting high heels. During high tides, the sea actually swallows up some of the streets closest to the port, temporarily transforming them into tropical Venetian canals. While tides and rainwater can leave the streets slippery, they also keep them clean.

The best way to explore Paraty is by wandering. Among the town's most handsome *sobrados* (mansions) is the **Casa da Cultura** (Rua Dona Geralda 177, tel. 24/3371-2325, www.casadaculturaparaty.org.br, 10am-10pm Tues.-Sun., R$8). Built in 1758, it hosts cultural events and has a permanent exhibition tracing Paraty's history. Several baroque churches are also particularly interesting; due to ongoing renovations, opening hours are in flux. The town's oldest church, **Igreja de Santa Rita dos Pardos Libertos** (Largo de Santa Rita, R$3), dates from 1722. Built by freed slaves, its interior houses a small collection of religious artifacts. Constructed a few years later, **Igreja Nossa Senhora do Rosário** (Rua do Comércio) was built by and for Paraty's slave population but is the only church in town with gold decoration on its altars, added in the 20th century. Paraty's principal and most grandiose church, **Igreja Matriz de Nossa Senhora de Remédios** (Praça da Matriz, R$2) was where the bourgeoisie worshipped. Outside on the Praça da Matriz is a small, daily crafts market selling local handicrafts. The town's aristocrats held their services in the late 18th-century **Igreja Nossa Senhora das Dores** (Rua Fresca), which has a privileged view of the sea and access to cooling breezes.

Venturing outside the *centro histórico,* take a 15-minute walk past Praia do Pontal to reach the **Forte Defensor Perpétuo** (9am-noon

cobblestoned street in colonial Paraty

and 2pm-5pm Tues.-Sun, R$2). This fortress was built in 1703 to prevent Paraty's gold from being hijacked by pirates. Restored in 1822, it houses a small museum with a display of local artisanal objects.

Beaches

Paraty is rich in beaches: Some 300 can be found along the surrounding coastline and among some 65 islands. Most beaches can be visited by boat leaving from Paraty's Cais de Porto; those along the coastline can be reached by car or, to a lesser extent, bus. Although the town has its own beaches, they aren't that attractive. The closest, **Praia do Pontal,** is a 10-minute walk from the *centro histórico.* While its beach *barraca* scene is lively, swimming isn't recommended. Cleaner and more deserted are **Praia do Forte** and **Praia do Jabaquara,** a wide beach whose shallow waters are ideal for bathing and kayaking.

Some of the finest and most easily accessible beaches are at **Trindade,** a fishing village and former hippie hangout 25 kilometers

(16 mi) south of Paraty along the Rio-Santos highway that can easily be reached by hourly local Colitur buses (R$3.70, 45 min.) departing from Paraty's bus terminal. To the east, the stunningly wild beaches of **Cepilho** and **Brava** are ideal for surfing, while to the west **Praia do Meio** and **Praia Cachadaço** (also good for snorkeling) are prized for their calm waters and natural swimming pools. You can get to Cachadaço by a 20-minute hike through the forest or by boat from Praia do Meio. Trindade's most far-flung beaches—**Praia do Sono** and **Praia dos Antigos**—are gloriously unspoiled. Reaching them entails a 2-3-hour hike or 20-30 minute boat ride.

Located 18 kilometers (11 mi) southwest of Paraty (8 km/5 mi are on an unpaved road) is **Paraty-Mirim,** with a lovely bay and invitingly calm waters as well as beach *barracas* reachable by municipal Colitur bus (R$3.70, 45 min.) or by boat. From here, it's only a 30-minute boat journey to **Saco do Mamanguá,** a narrow, 8-kilometer (5-mi) bay that hides 30 completely deserted beaches. From Paraty, it's possible to organize an outing that includes canoeing and hiking.

Boat Excursions

Various schooners offer five-hour trips around Paraty's bay with stops at islands such as **Ilha Comprida** (known for its diving) as well as otherwise inaccessible and enticing beaches such as **Praia da Lula** and **Praia Vermelha.** Lunch is included, as are caipirinhas (and sometimes rambunctious live music that might grate on those who imagined a more bucolic outing). For information, contact **Paraty Tours** (Av. Roberto Silveira 11, tel. 24/3371-1327, www.paratytours.com.br), which also organizes kayaking, horseback riding, and hiking trips. A five-hour tour costs R$40 pp. Individuals and small groups can charter boats at an hourly rate (7-15 people, R$30-50 pp) from the *barqueiros* at Cais de Porto.

Trekking

At the **Associação de Guias de Turismo de Paraty** (tel. 24/3371-1783, R$130 pp per day, accommodations and food not included), individuals and small groups can hire guides to travel the forested coastline to secluded beaches, including those around Saco do Mamanguá, with stops for bathing in bays and waterfalls. An enticing journey is to follow the **Caminho do Ouro,** the route along which gold was transported over the mountains from Minas to Paraty during colonial times. The historical hike along a 2-kilometer (1.2-mi) stretch of irregular cobblestones can be done in the company of a guide from the **Centro de Informações Turísticas Caminho do Ouro** (Estrada Paraty-Cunha, tel. 24/3371-1222, 9am-noon and 2pm-5pm Wed.-Sun., R$25) as well as with ecotour agencies. Operated by an Irish transplant, **Paraty Explorer** (tel. 24/9952-4496, www.paratyexplorer.com) is an exceptional outfit that specializes in hiking trips as well as kayak and paddleboard outings—book a half-day outing (R$35-50) to the Caminho do Ouro with a time-out for waterfall plunging and cachaça sampling.

Entertainment and Events

Paraty has a vibrant and cosmopolitan nightlife and cultural scene, although most of the action takes place during the summer or July, and on weekends.

NIGHTLIFE

Charming bars with live music are concentrated along Rua Marechal Deodoro in Paraty. A traditional favorite with a loyal following, **Margarida Café** (Praça do Chafariz, tel. 24/3371-6037, www.margaridacafe.com.br, noon-midnight daily, R$25-35) is an atmospheric restaurant-bar; they feature live jazz and MPB every night. **Paraty 33** (Rua da Lapa 357, tel. 24/3371-7311, www.paraty33.com.br) has a low-key tavern atmosphere and lures a younger, more animated crowd. Beer lovers should visit the **Cervejaria Caborê** (Av. Otávio Gama 420, Caborê, tel. 24/3371-2248, www.cervejariacabore.com.br, 5pm-midnight Wed.-Fri., noon-midnight

Sat.-Sun.), a microbrewery where you can check out the production facilities and then sample the wares at the in-house pub.

You don't have to understand Portuguese to be enchanted by the plays performed by the Contadores de Estórias at the Teatro de Bonecos (Rua Dona Geralda 327, tel. 24/3371-1575, www.ecparaty.org.br, 9pm Wed. and Sat. year-round, plus 9pm Fri. Jan.-Feb. and July, R$50). This renowned troupe of actors are talented manipulators of a disarmingly lifelike cast of doll-like puppets (*bonecos*) who mutely act out poignant and hilarious dramatic sketches. Leave the kids (under 14) at home, since these puppet shows are for adults only, and buy tickets in advance.

FESTIVALS

Carnaval is a serious street party; a highlight is the Bloco da Lama (www.blocodalama.com.br), composed of mud-covered young things dancing through the streets.

Paraty comes alive in the winter months (May-Aug.) for several popular *festas*. The Festa do Divino takes place 40 days after Easter and lasts for two weeks. This colorful religious festival hosts parades and celebrations along with theatrical, dance, and musical performances that take place in the street. Also known for their ornate pageantry are Semana Santa (Easter) and Corpus Christi (June). Since 2009, a top-notch roster of international artists has lured jazz lovers to town for the Bourbon Festival Paraty (www.bourbonfestivalparaty.com.br) during the last week in May. During the third weekend in August, *cachaça* lovers from far and wide descend on the town for the Festival da Pinga. Not just for bookworms, the Festa Literária Internacional (FLIP, www.flip.org.br), which takes place for five days in August, lures more visitors to Paraty than Carnaval. Readings and debates are attended by the likes of Paul Auster, Salman Rushdie, Margaret Atwood, and Ian McEwan, and the town comes alive with cultural and culinary happenings.

Shopping

Paraty is famous for its *cachaças,* produced in the surrounding region. One of the most potent brands is Corisco; Paratiana and Maria Izabel are smoother and more discreet. At *cachaça* boutiques, you can sample the wares even if you don't want to purchase; try Armazém da Cachaça (Rua do Comércio, tel. 24/3371-7519) and Empório da Cachaça (Rua Dr. Samuel da Costa 22, tel. 24/3371-6329). You can also visit many of the *alambiques* (distilleries); many have been in operation for generations and are located relatively close to town. One of the better tours is to Maria Izabel (BR-101 Km. 568, Sítio Antonio, Corumbé, tel. 24/9999-9908, www.mariaizabel.com.br). Respected and artisanal, it is also the only *alambique* owned and operated by a woman, Maria Izabel Gibrail Costa. Advance reservations are necessary.

Paraty is full of ateliers and boutiques flaunting an endless variety of objets d'art. Among the most unique and hard to resist are the miniature *caiçara* fishing vessels, made from wood and painted in vibrant colors, sold at Atelier da Terra (Rua da Lapa 1, tel. 24/3371-3070).

Accommodations

In the summer and during holidays (including Carnaval, the Festival da Pinga, and the Festa Literária Internacional), finding a room can be tricky, so reserve in advance. You'll have more luck and cheaper rates at one of the many newer places outside the *centro histórico;* try the *bairros* of Caborê and Chácara or Jabaquara beach or nearby Trindade, where hostels have mushroomed. If you have a car, take advantage of many idyllic spots tucked away in the forest-clad mountains. During the off-season (particularly weekdays), you can often negotiate rate reductions of up to 30-40 percent.

One of the most attractive and affordable hotels in the *centro histórico* is the Solar do Gerânios (Praça da Matriz, tel. 24/3371-1550, www.paraty.com.br/geranio, R$120-160 d), which offers a homey atmosphere enhanced by the friendly owner and her cats. Guest rooms are small but spotless and cheery; the best ones have small balconies overlooking the square. Lacking in historic character, yet quaint and friendly, **Pousada Flor do Mar** (Rua Fresca 257, tel. 24/3371-1674, www. pousadaflordomar.com.br, R$190-220 d) is another good choice that offers clean and colorfully painted guest rooms.

Highly atmospheric, **Pousada do Ouro** (Rua da Praia 145, tel. 24/3371-4300, www. pousadaouro.com.br, R$370-480 d) possesses tastefully furnished colonial-style guest rooms in a beautiful 18th-century *sobrado* (and a less impressive annex). A sauna, fitness room, and pool round out the amenities. One of Paraty's oldest guesthouses, **Pousada Pardieiro** (Rua do Comércio 74, tel. 24/3371-1370, www.pousadapardieiro. com.br, no children under age 15, R$310-420 d) clusters 18th-century houses converted into apartments. Guest rooms are impeccably furnished and face a pool and tranquil gardens.

Upon arriving at the **Pousada de Arte Urquijo** (Rua Dona Geralda 79, tel. 24/3371-1362, www.urquijo.com.br, no children under age 12, R$420-590 d), guests are invited to remove their shoes and don comfortable Japanese slippers in which they can glide around the polished wood floors of this uniquely renovated 18th-century *sobrado*. Painter-proprietor Luz Urquijo has an artist's eye for detail, reflected in the unusual furnishings and bright bold canvases on the walls (many by Luz and her daughter).

Although it's a 10-minute walk from the *centro histórico*, distance is a small price to pay for the exceptional comfort and privacy at ★ **Vivenda** (Rua Beija-Flor 9, Caborê, tel. 24/3371-4272, www.vivendaparaty.com, R$320-370 d). Accommodations consist of two modern but exquisitely designed and decorated bungalows and an apartment, which look out onto a pool and garden. English owner and host John makes visitors feel as if they are house guests, with the result that

checking out is like leaving a second home. Also in Caborê is **Music Art Hostel** (Rua Rita Ribeiro da Gama, Caborê, tel. 24/3371-8345, www.musicarthostel.com, R$140 d, R$40 pp), offers performances, live music jams, and *festas*. Dorms, private rooms, and a large communal kitchen are scattered among a colonial house with lofty ceilings, vast shuttered windows, and a pool. Bikes are available for rent (R$5), and an on-site restaurant-bar slakes thirst and hunger.

Food

The majority of Paraty's restaurants occupy charming *sobrados* in the *centro histórico*. *Caiçara* is the name given to local specialties that draw on fish, game, fruits, and vegetables traditionally used by the Costa Verde's indigenous peoples.

Banana da Terra (Rua Dr. Samuel Costa 198, tel. 24/3371-1725, www.restaurantebananadaterra.com.br, 6pm-midnight Mon. and Wed.-Thurs., noon-4pm and 7pm-midnight Fri.-Sun. Mar.-Nov., noon-midnight daily Dec.-Feb., R$50-70) serves up *caiçara* fare with a touch of refinement prepared by Ana Bueno, considered one of Brazil's top chefs. True to its name, various varieties of bananas make frequent appearances on the (somewhat overpriced) menu in guises both savory (banana-and-cheese-stuffed squid gratiné with shrimp) and sweet (warm banana tart with cinnamon ice cream).

The location of **Sabor da Terra** (Av. Roberto Silveira 180, tel. 24/3371-2384, www. paraty.com.br/sabordaterra, 11am-10pm daily, R$15-25), just outside the *centro histórico*, may justify the low-wattage decor and equally low prices. However, this per-kilo restaurant earns high marks in terms of the variety, freshness, and tastiness of its buffet offerings. Another inexpensive option is **Le Castellet** (Rua Dona Geralda 44, tel. 24/3371-4649, http://lecastelletyveslepide.com.br, 6pm-midnight Tues.-Fri., noon-midnight Sat.-Sun., R$20-35). Chef Yves Lapide has outfitted this cozy little *crêperie* with attractive decorative touches from his native Provence, but his real forte is delicious sweet and savory crepes, along with other French fare.

Casa do Fogo (Rua Comendador José Luiz 390, tel. 24/3371-3163, www.casadofogo.com.br, 6pm-1am Thurs.-Tues., R$30-55) takes its name literally: A majority of its main dishes (even desserts and drinks) arrive at the table on fire (*fogo*). Taking advantage of the local *cachaça* supply, local chef "Caju" flambées everything from shrimp (served with guava rice) to mangoes and star fruit (served with passion fruit jelly). The romantic atmosphere is abetted by nightly performances of chorinho and MPB.

For centuries, many escaped and freed slaves fled into remote rural regions of Brazil, where they created their own settlements and maintained cultural and religious vestiges passed down from their African ancestors. Today, there are thousands of *quilombos* throughout Brazil, including **Quilombo do Campinho** (http://quilombocampinhodaindependencia.blogspot.com). Located just south of Paraty, off the Rio-Santos highway, this traditional community of 120 families is home to ★ **Restaurante do Quilombo** (BR-101 Km. 589, tel. 24/3871-4866, 11am-5pm daily, R$15-30), a community-operated restaurant. The emphasis is on fresh fish and locally farmed produce; portions are robust and prices are honest. You can explore the community via guided tours (R$20) given by residents.

COOKING CLASSES

Treat yourself to a night of cooking (and eating) at the **Academia de Cozinha e Outros Prazeres** (Rua Dona Geralda 288, tel. 24/3371-6468, www.chefbrasil.com, R$190). The "Academy of Cooking and Other Pleasures" is run by Yara Costa Roberts, a professional chef whose fluent English is a result of years spent in the United States. Several nights a week, Yara offers small groups a chance to learn how to prepare dishes from Bahia, the Amazon, the Cerrado region (in the Central-West), and her own home state of Minas Gerais.

Transportation and Services

The **Centro de Informações Turísticas** (Av. Roberto Silveira 1, tel. 24/3371-1222, 8am-8pm daily), located at the entrance to the *centro histórico,* has maps, bus schedules to other beaches, and other information. Two useful bilingual websites with lots of information are www.paraty.com.br and www.paraty.tur.br.

Viação Costa Verde (tel. 21/3622-3123, www.costaverdetransportes.com.br) offers almost hourly daily bus departures from 4am-9pm between Rio and Paraty (4.5 hours, R$63). **Viação Reunidas** (tel. 0300/210-3000, www.reunidaspaulista.com.br) offers four daily departures from 8am-10:30pm between São Paulo's Rodoviária Tietê and Paraty (6 hours, R$52). The Rodoviária (Rua Jango Pádua) is 500 meters (0.3 mi) from the *centro histórico.*

By car from Rio, simply follow BR-101, the Rio-Santos highway (236 km/147 mi). From São Paulo, take the Rodovia Ayrton Senna and then the Mogi-Bertioga highway to BR 101 and drive north to Paraty (338 km/210 mi). An alternative route is to take the Ayrton Senna to the Rodovia Carvalho Pinto and then take the Rodovia dos Tamoios to BR-101 (285 km/177 mi).

From Rio, **Easy Transfer** (tel. 21/9386-3919, www.easytransferbrazil.com) operates vans that pick you up at your hotel and take you all the way to Paraty (R$90, 5 hours).

Photo Credits

MAP SYMBOLS

≡≡≡ Expressway	○ City/Town	✈ Airport	⌁ Golf Course
— Primary Road	◉ State Capital	✖ Airfield	P Parking Area
— Secondary Road	⊛ National Capital	▲ Mountain	≜ Archaeological Site
⋯ Unpaved Road	★ Point of Interest	✛ Unique Natural Feature	⌂ Church
— Feature Trail	• Accommodation		⛽ Gas Station
----- Other Trail	▼ Restaurant/Bar	⌇ Waterfall	Glacier
⋯⋯ Ferry	■ Other Location	▲ Park	Mangrove
Pedestrian Walkway	▲ Campground	❶ Trailhead	Reef
⊞⊞⊞ Stairs		✖ Skiing Area	Swamp

CONVERSION TABLES

$°C = (°F - 32) / 1.8$
$°F = (°C \times 1.8) + 32$
1 inch = 2.54 centimeters (cm)
1 foot = 0.304 meters (m)
1 yard = 0.914 meters
1 mile = 1.6093 kilometers (km)
1 km = 0.6214 miles
1 fathom = 1.8288 m
1 chain = 20.1168 m
1 furlong = 201.168 m
1 acre = 0.4047 hectares
1 sq km = 100 hectares
1 sq mile = 2.59 square km
1 ounce = 28.35 grams
1 pound = 0.4536 kilograms
1 short ton = 0.90718 metric ton
1 short ton = 2,000 pounds
1 long ton = 1.016 metric tons
1 long ton = 2,240 pounds
1 metric ton = 1,000 kilograms
1 quart = 0.94635 liters
1 US gallon = 3.7854 liters
1 Imperial gallon = 4.5459 liters
1 nautical mile = 1.852 km

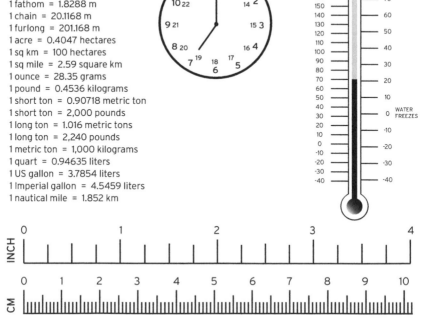

MOON SPOTLIGHT RIO DE JANEIRO
Avalon Travel
a member of the Perseus Books Group
1700 Fourth Street
Berkeley, CA 94710, USA
www.moon.com

Editor: Sabrina Young
Series Manager: Kathryn Ettinger
Copy Editor: Kristie Reilley
Graphics and Production Coordinator:
   Lucie Ericksen
Map Editor: Kat Bennett
Cartographer: Stephanie Poulain

ISBN-13: 978-1-61238-936-3

Front cover photo: view from Corcovado to Sugarloaf Mountain, Rio de Janeiro © studio157 | istockphoto.com

Printed in the United States

About the Author

Michael Sommers

Born in Texas and raised in Toronto, Michael Sommers grew up with travel on the brain – a consequence of time spent riding around in Oldsmobiles, Mini Mokes, and Pan Am jets in the company of a Gourmet-addicted mother and a father with a roving zoom lens.

When Michael turned 18 he took flight, setting down temporary roots in cities such as Bordeaux, Paris, Montreal, New York, and Lisbon. During this time, he earned a BA in Literature from McGill University and an MA in History and Civilizations from the École des Hautes Études en Sciences Sociales, where his thesis was "The Image of Brazil and Brazilians in Hollywood Cinema." He also worked as a writer and editor at magazines and newspapers and freelanced for publications such as *The New York Times, The International Herald Tribune,* and *The Globe and Mail.*

Michael first traveled to Brazil at the age of four. His only memory is being served a glistening orange wedge of papaya in the grand dining room at Rio de Janeiro's Hotel Gloria. Twenty years later, he returned to Brazil, where he was seduced by the intense, colorful landscapes, rich cultures, and warm people. Michael eventually settled down in Salvador, the baroque capital of Bahia, where he has worked as a writer and journalist for more than 15 years.

While Michael has yet to master the art of preparing *feijoada* (Brazil's national stew of beans, salted beef, and pork), he does make a mean *caipirinha.*

CPSIA information can be obtained at www.ICGtesting.com
Printed in the USA
LVOW01s0849250615

443838LV00003B/5/P